G000153495

Boston

must
SEES

Chief Editor	Cynthia Clayton Ochterbeck
Senior Editor	Gwen Cannon
Writers	Diane Bair and Pamela Wright
Production Coordinator	Allison M. Simpson
Cartography	Peter Wrenn
Photo Editor	Brigitta L. House
Documentation	Martha Hunt, Doug Rogers
Typesetting	Octavo Design
	Apopka, Florida
Cover Design	Paris Venise Design
	Paris, 17e
Printing and Binding	Colonial Press International, Inc.
	Miami, Florida

Contact us:
Michelin North America
One Parkway South
Greenville, SC 29615
USA
800-423-0485
www.michelin-us.com
email: TheGreenGuide-us@us.michelin.com

Special Sales:

For information regarding bulk sales, customized editions and premium sales, please contact our Customer Service Departments:

USA – 800-423-0485   **Canada** – 800-361-8236

Manufacture française des pneumatiques Michelin

Société en commandite par actions au capital de 304 000 000 EUR
Place des Carmes-Déchaux – 63 Clermont-Ferrand (France)
R.C.S. Clermont-FD B 855 800 507

© Michelin et Cie, Propriétaires-éditeurs, 2005
Dépôt légal avril 2005 – ISBN 2-067-11120-5
Printed in 04-05/ 1.1

Note to the reader:

While every effort is made to ensure that all information in this guide is correct and up-to-date, Michelin Travel Publications (Michelin North America, Inc.) accepts no liability for any direct, indirect or consequential losses howsoever caused so far as such can be excluded by law.

Admission prices listed for sights in this guide are for a single adult, unless otherwise specified.

Welcome to Boston

Table of Contents

Table of Contents

Map List

THE MICHELIN STARS

For more than 75 years, travelers have used the Michelin stars to take the guesswork out of planning a trip. Our star-rating system helps you make the best decision on where to go, what to do, and what to see. A three-star rating means it's one of the "absolutelys"; two stars means it's one of the "should sees"; and one star says it's one of the "sees"—a must if you have the time.

★★★	Absolutely Must See
★★	Really Must See
★	Must See

Three-Star Sights

Boston Symphony Orchestra★★★
Cape Cod National Seashore★★★
Faneuil Hall★★★
Freedom Trail★★★
Harvard University★★★
Isabella Stewart Gardner Museum★★★
Museum of Fine Arts, Boston★★★
Nantucket★★★
Old North Church★★★
Old Sturbridge Village★★★
Peabody Essex Museum★★★

Two-Star Sights

Back Bay★★
Beacon Hill★★
Boston Center for the Arts★★
Boston Children's Museum★★
Boston Museum of Science★★
Boston Pops★★
Boston Public Garden★★
Boston Public Library★★
Cambridge★★
Cape Ann★★
Christian Science Center★★
City Hall★★
Commonwealth Avenue★★
Concord★★
Copley Square★★
Faneuil Hall Marketplace★★
Fenway Park★★

John Hancock Tower★★
Lexington★★
Louisburg Square★★
Martha's Vineyard★★
Mayflower II★★
Newbury Street★★
New England Aquarium★★
Old South Meeting House★★
Old State House★★
Plimoth Plantation★★
Plymouth★★
Provincetown★★
Salem★★
State House★★
Singing Beach★★
Trinity Church★★
USS Constitution★★

One-Star Sights

African Meeting House★
Arnold Arboretum★
Back Bay Fens★
Beacon Street★
Boston Athenaeum★
Boston Common★
Brewster★
Charles River Esplanade★
Charlestown★
Copp's Hill
   Burying Ground★
Edgartown★
First Baptist
   Church of Boston★
Fogg Art Museum★
Forest Hills Cemetery★
Gibson House Museum★
Gloucester★
Heritage Museums
   and Gardens★
John F. Kennedy
   Library and Museum★
King's Chapel★
King's Chapel
   Burying Ground★

Longfellow National
   Historic Site★
Massachusetts Institute
   of Technology★
Minute Man
   National Historical Park★
MIT Museum★
Nichols House Museum★
North End★
Old Granary
   Burying Ground★
Park Street Church★
Paul Revere House★
Plymouth Rock★
Revere Beach★
Robert Gould
   Shaw Memorial★
Rockport★
Sackler Museum★
Salem Maritime
   National Historic Site★
Sandwich★
South End★
Waterfront★

Listed below is a selection of the Boston area's most popular annual events. Please note that dates may change from year to year. For more detailed information, call the citywide events hotline at 617-635-3911 or the Mayor's Office of Tourism at 617-635-4447. On the Web visit www.bostonusa.com or www.cityofboston.gov/calendar.

January

Chinese New Year (late Jan–Feb)   617-635-4447
Chinatown   www.cityofboston.gov/calendar

February

Chocolate and Ice Sculpture Festival   978-740-1208
Downtown & Pickering Wharf, Salem
                        www.salemmainstreets.org

Hasty Pudding Theatricals (Feb–Mar)   617-495-5205
10 Holyoke St., Harvard University, Cambridge
                        www.hastypudding.org

March

New England Spring Flower Show   617-933-4970
Bayside Exposition Center   www.masshort.org

St. Patrick's Day Parade   617-635-3911
Broadway St., South Boston
                        www.cityofboston.gov/calendar

April

Boston Marathon   617-236-1652
Hopkinton to Boston (Beacon & Commonwealth Sts.)
                        www.bostonmarathon.com

Boston Red Sox Opening Day   877-733-7699
Fenway Park, 4 Yawkey Way, Back Bay
                        www.redsox.com

Hatch Shell Earth Day Concert   617-931-1111
Charles River Esplanade   www.cityofboston.gov/arts

Nantucket Daffodil Festival   508-228-1700
Various locations, Nantucket
                        www.nantucketchamber.org

Patriots' Day   781-862-2480
Various locations, Lexington and Concord
                        www.lexingtonchamber.org

May

Arts First – Cambridge   617-495-8699
Harvard University, Cambridge www.fas.harvard.edu/~arts

Beacon Hill Hidden Gardens Tour   617-227-4392
Beacon Hill   (call for advance reservations)

Cape Cod Maritime Days   888-332-3225
Various locations   www.CapeCodChamber.org

Duckling Day Parade (Mother's Day)   617-426-1885
Boston Common   www.bostonusa.com

Kite & Flight Festival   617-635-4032
Franklin Park Golf Course, Dorchester
                        www.cityofboston.gov/parks

June

Boston Harborfest (late Jun–early Jul) 617-227-1528
Boston Harbor and City Hall Plaza
www.bostonharborfest.com

Dragon Boat Festival 617-426-6500
Charles River near Harvard University, Cambridge
www.bostondragonboat.org

Provincetown International Film Festival 508-487-3456
Various locations, Provincetown
www.ptownfilmfest.org

July

Annual Salem Maritime Festival 978-740-1660
Historic Waterfront, Salem www.salem.org

Boston Pops – 617-267-2400
Pop Goes the 4th Concert & Fireworks
Hatch Shell at The Esplanade www.july4th.org

North End Italian Feast Days (Jul–late Aug) 617-635-3911
North End www.cityofboston.gov/arts

August

August Moon Festival 617-542-2574
Chinatown www.bostonusa.com

Boston Antique & Classic Boat Festival 617-422-1703
Hawthorne Cove Marina, 10 White St., Salem
www.northofboston.org

Cambridge Carnival Internationale 617-492-2518
Massachusetts Ave., Cambridge
www.cambridgecarnival.com

September

Boston Arts Festival 617-635-3911
Christopher Columbus Park, Waterfront
www.bostonusa.com

October

Haunted Happenings 877-725-3662
Various locations, Salem www.salem.org

The Head of the Charles Regatta 617-886-6200
Charles River, Cambridge www.hocr.org

Oktoberfest in Harvard Square 617-491-3434
Harvard Square, Cambridge www.harvardsquare.com

November

Boston Antiquarian Book Fair 617-266-6540
Hynes Convention Center www.bostonbookfair.com

Thanksgiving at Plimoth Plantation 508-746-1622
Plimoth Plantation, Plymouth www.plimoth.org

December

Enchanted Village 617-635-3689
Hynes Convention Center www.cityofboston.gov

First Night Boston 617-542-1399
Various locations www.firstnight.org

Must Know: Practical Information

WHEN TO GO TO BOSTON

Boston offers year-round incentives for a visit, but most tourists descend upon the city from May through October. The summer stretch brims with sun-drenched concerts, cruises and cafes; heat and humidity give way to crisp, dry air in early October, when trees burst with color, universities pulse with re-turning students, and hotels overflow with guests. The surge levels out by late October, when cool weather and lower room rates provide a window of oppor-tunity for savvy visitors. Come November, winter light casts a cozy glow on red brick around the city, as Christmas shopping—and, often, snow—keep the hustle and bustle indoors. Freezing temperatures remain through February, but March welcomes the first signs of spring with temperatures in the fifties (March and November are among the rainiest months). Sightseers of a different breed pack the city in April, when the Boston Marathon attracts large numbers of participants and spectators.

Seasonal Temperatures in Boston

	Jan	Apr	July	Oct
Avg. high	36°F / 2°C	54°F / 12°C	80°F / 27°C	62°F / 17°C
Avg. low	20°F / -7°C	38°F / 3°C	63°F / 17°C	46°F /8°C

PLANNING YOUR TRIP

Before you go, contact the following agencies to obtain maps and information about sightseeing, accommodations, travel packages, recreational opportunities and seasonal events.

Greater Boston Convention & Visitors Bureau
2 Copley Place, Suite 105, Boston, MA 02116
617-536-4100 or 800-888-5515; www.bostonusa.com.

Cambridge Tourism Office
4 Brattle Street, Cambridge, MA 02138
617-441-2884 or 800-862-5678; www.cambridge-usa.org.

Cape Cod Convention & Visitors Bureau
Route 6 at Route 132, Hyannis, MA 02601
508-362-3225 or 888-332-2732; www.capecodchamber.com.

Visitor Information Centers

Boston Common Visitor Information Center
140 Tremont St., at West St.; 617-451-2227
Open year-round Mon–Sat 8:30am–5pm, Sun 9am–5pm.

Prudential Center Visitor Information Center
800 Boyleston St.
Open Mon–Sat 8:30am–5pm.

National Park Service Visitor Center
15 State St.; 617-242-5642; www.nps.gov/bost
Open year-round daily 9am–5pm. Closed Jan 1, Thanksgiving Day & Dec 25.

Web Sites

Here are some additional Web sites to help you plan your trip:
www.boston-online.com
www.mass-vacation.com
www.bostonchefs.com
(lists current menu of area restaurants)
www.bostoncitysearch.com
(lists entertainment and restaurant reviews)

CityPass – Consider buying a CityPass booklet *($39 adults; $19.50 children ages 3-11; good for a full year)*, which gives you a substantially discounted admission to the following attractions: Museum of Science, New England Aquarium, Skywalk Observatory, Museum of Fine Arts, Harvard Museum of Natural History and John F. Kennedy Library and Museum. You can buy your CityPass from the **Greater Boston Convention & Visitors Bureau** *(opposite)*, at any of the participating attractions, or online at www.citypass.com.

In the News

Boston's two main daily morning newspapers are the *Boston Globe (www.boston.com)* and the *BostonHerald (www.bostonherald.com)*. Both offer arts and entertainment supplements: the Globe's is published on Sunday while the Herald supplement, *The Edge*, is published daily. The weekly alternative paper, *Boston Phoenix (www.bostonphoenix.com)*, published on Thursday, offers a different perspective of the city as well as good coverage of the arts and nightlife. Check out the monthly *Boston* magazine for its annual Best of Boston list. Got kids in tow? Be in the know with the *Boston Parents Paper*, a great resource for events to entertain the young ones. The publication is available in many kid-friendly locations such as libraries, supermarkets and museums.

GETTING TO BOSTON

By Air – Both domestic and international flights service **Logan International Airport (BOS)**, located 2 miles northeast of downtown *(from Boston, take the Callahan Tunnel to the second exit for the airport; from the south, take the Ted Williams Tunnel to the airport; 617-428-2800; www.massport.com/logan)*.

Shuttles – Free shuttle-bus service between terminals is available at arrival levels, the airport subway station on the **Massachusetts Bay Transportation Authority (MBTA)** Blue Line, the Water Transportation Terminal and satellite parking. The service runs seven days a week; call or visit the airport Web site for schedules. A number of companies offer transportation from the airport to downtown hotels by **shared van**, which averages $12 per person *(for a list of companies, check online at www.massport.com/logan)*. **Water taxis** *(see sidebar, below)* also service Logan airport.

Subway – The MBTA Blue Line services Logan Airport *(see p 13)*.

Airport Taxis – Taxi service from the airport to downtown averages $15 to $20, plus a $1.50 fee and a $4.50 harbor-tunnel toll. *For a list of metered rates from Boston hotels and suburbs to the airport, check online at www.massport.com/logan/getti.html.*

Boston Water Taxi

Take the road (or wave) less traveled and experience taxi service via boat! Massport courtesy bus service runs from the arrival terminals directly to the Logan dock; from there, you can hop aboard the MBTA Harbor Express, which offers a full schedule of daily connections between Logan, Long Wharf and the South Shore. The nautical trip across the harbor offers heated/air-conditioned cabins, as well as telephones and food and beverage service. Vessels are wheelchair accessible. *For schedules and rates, call 617-222-6999 or check online at www.harborexpress.com.*

Must Know: Practical Information

By Train – **Amtrak** trains leave from South Station, in the Financial District, Downtown *(Atlantic Ave. & Summer St.; 800-872-7245; www.amtrak.com)*. Suburban MBTA trains depart from South Station and North Station *(150 Causeway St.)* in the North End. *For schedules and fares, call 617-222-3200 or check online at www.mbta.com.*

By Bus – Boston's main bus terminal is located at South Station *(617-330-1230)*. For fares, schedules and routes, call 800-229-9424 or visit www.greyhound.com.

By Car – Boston can easily be accessed from a number of major highways: I-95 circumvents the city on the west, I-90 enters from the west, and I-93 forms the north-south corridor through the city.

GETTING AROUND BOSTON

By Car – If you have the choice, don't drive in Boston. Downtown streets weave, wind and end, according to no set or sane pattern. Street signs may change from block to block: Winter turns into Summer, Court into State, Kneeland into Stuart. Between the volume of traffic, the aggressive drivers, and the constant detours caused by Big Dig construction *(p 43)*, driving can be a hassle here, to say the least.

If you must drive in Boston, avoid the roads during commuter rush hours *(weekdays 7:30am–9am and 4pm–6pm)*. You will want a car for visiting the surrounding areas as well as Cape Cod. Use of seat belts is required. Child safety seats are mandatory for children 4 years old or younger or 40 pounds or less.

Parking – Street parking is generally difficult, adding another deterrent to driving in Boston. If you decide to brave the roads, however, garages at Boston Common, John Hancock Tower and Prudential Center are all operational 24 hours a day.

> **Touring Tip**
>
> The infamous Big Dig has generally improved the flow of traffic in and out of the city: lanes and on- and off-ramps have been added, and there's direct access from the airport and from the north and south freeways. That said, you'll still find traffic snarls and detours during the final phases of construction. *For up-to-date information on Big Dig construction as well as city driving tips, visit www.masspike.com/bigdig/index.html or www.smartraveler.com.*

Safety Tips

Although muggings are rare in Boston, visitors should remember these common-sense tips to ensure a safe and enjoyable visit:

- Exercise caution, and avoid visiting the Boston Common, The Fens and other wooded areas, as well as Charlestown, after dark. Steer clear of secluded streets and alleyways, even in pretty neighborhoods like Beacon Hill and the South End.
- Stay awake when riding public transportation. Avoid empty subway cars and deserted station hallways and platforms after 9pm (consider taking a cab after dark).
- Avoid carrying large sums of money, and don't let strangers see how much money you're carrying.
- Keep a firm hold on purses and knapsacks, carry your wallet in your front pocket and avoid wearing expensive jewelry.
- Always park your car in a well-lit area. Close windows, lock doors and place valuables in the trunk.

Rates run the gamut from $6/hour to $35/day, while some facilities give "early-bird" discounts (25%) for those who park before 10:30am.

By Foot – Walking is one of the best ways to explore Boston. The Back Bay, Beacon Hill, Downtown and the North End are all easy areas to navigate on foot. In fact, that's the best way to take in the wonderful architecture, shopping and other sites.

By Public Transportation – The **Massachusetts Bay Transportation Authority (MBTA)** operates an extensive network of subways, elevated trains and trolleys *(617-222-3200 or 800-392-6100; www.mbta.com)*. **Peter Pan Bus Lines** *(800-343-9999; www.peterpanbus.com)*, based at South Station, provides bus services to cities in Massachusetts, Connecticut, New Hampshire and New York.

Take a Trolley Tour

So what if you look like a tourist? Grab your camera and hop aboard one of Boston's popular trolley tours. They're actually quite informative and a good bet in rainy or humid summer weather. **The Red Beantown Trolley** *(800-343-1328; www.brushhilltours.com/tours/beantown.htm)*, **Boston Trolley Tours** *(617-742-2194; www.discoverbostontours.com)*, and **Old Town Trolley** *(617-269-7010; www.historictours.com/boston)* essentially offer the same tours, with unlimited re-boarding throughout the day.

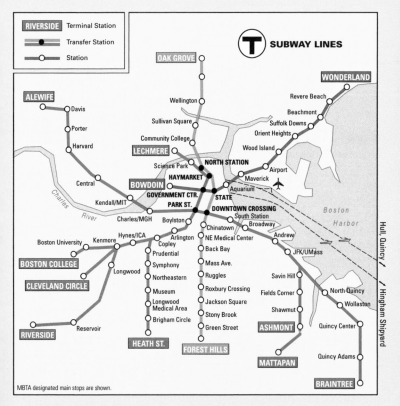

Must Know: Practical Information

MBTA Commuter Rail Line – Known to locals as the "T," this rail line links Boston with Providence, Worcester, Lowell, Haverhill, Newburyport, Rockport, Concord, Norfolk, Plymouth and surrounding areas. Fares depend on the distance traveled, and range from $1.25 to $6. Children under 5 years of age travel free-of-charge, and half-fares apply to children ages 5 to 11, junior high and high school students, senior citizens and persons with disabilities. Trains generally operate between 5am and 1am *(for schedules and fares, contact MBTA: 617-222-3200; www.mbta.com)*.

By Taxi – Cabs are readily available at all hours in Boston; you can hail cabs on the street, or find them outside major hotels. Rates within the city start at $1.50, then 25¢ for the first quarter-mile and 25¢ for every eighth of a mile. If you plan to travel to or from the airport or suburbs, flat rates apply outside the 12-mile downtown radius. Major cab companies include:

Ambassador Brattle Cab – 617-492-1100; www.brattlecourier.com.

Boston Cab Association – 617-536-3200.

Cambridge Checker Cab – 617-497-1500.

Checker – 617-536-7000.

Green Cab Association – 617-628-0600.

Independent Taxi Operators Association (ITOA) – 617-426-8700; www.itoataxi.com.

Town Taxi – 617-536-5000; www.towntaxiboston.com.

AREA CODES
To call between different area codes, dial 1 + area code + seven-digit number. The same applies to local calls, even within the same area code.

Boston & Cambridge: **617** and **857**
Boston Suburbs: **339** and **781**
Outlying Areas: **508** and **774** (southwest); **351** and **978** (northwest)
Cape Cod, Nantucket and Martha's Vineyard: **508**

Important Numbers	
Emergency police/ambulance/fire *(24hrs)*	911
Police *(non-emergency, Mon–Fri 9am–6pm)*	617-343-4200
Poison Control	617-232-2120
Medical Referral	617-726-5800
Dental Emergencies	508-651-3521
24-hour Pharmacies	
CVS – 587 Boylston St., Back Bay, Boston	617-437-8414
36 White St. at Somerville Ave., Cambridge	617-876-5519
Travelers Aid Society Hotline	617-635-4500
Time	617-637-1234
Weather	617-936-1234

TIPS FOR SPECIAL VISITORS

Disabled Travelers – Federal law requires that businesses (including hotels and restaurants) provide access for the disabled, devices for the hearing impaired, and designated parking spaces. For further information, contact the Society for

Accessible Travel and Hospitality (SATH), 347 Fifth Ave., Suite 610, New York NY 10016 *(212-447-7284; www.sath.org)*.

All national parks have facilities for the disabled, and offer free or discounted passes. For details, contact the National Park Service *(Office of Public Inquiries, P.O. Box 37127, Room 1013, Washington, DC 20013-7127; 202-208-4747; www.nps.gov)*.

Passengers who will need assistance with train or bus travel should give advance notice to Amtrak *(800-872-7245 or 800-523-6590/TDD; www.amtrak.com)* or Greyhound *(800-752-4841 or 800-345-3109/TDD; www.greyhound.com)*. Reservations for hand-controlled rental cars should be made in advance with the rental company.

Local Lowdown – For information about disabled access to public transportation, contact the **Massachusetts Bay Transportation Authority**: *617-222-3200 or 800-392-6100; www.mbta.com*. The following agencies also provide detailed information about access for the disabled in the Boston Area:

• **Boston Center for Independent Living** – 95 Berkeley St. 617-338-6665. www.bostoncil.org.
• **Boston Guild for the Hard of Hearing** – 617-254-7300/TTY.
• **Massachusetts Office on Disability** – 1 Ashburton Pl. 617-727-7440 or 800-322-2020/TTY. www.state.ma.us/mod.

Senior Citizens – Many hotels, attractions and restaurants offer discounts to visitors age 62 or older (proof of age may be required). The **AARP** (formerly American Association of Retired Persons) offers discounts to its members *(601 E St. NW, Washington, DC 20049; 202-424-3410; www.aarp.com)*.

FOREIGN VISITORS

Visitors from outside the US can obtain information from the Greater Boston Convention & Visitors Bureau *(617-536-4100 or 800-888-5515; www.bostonusa.com)* or from the US embassy or consulate in their country of residence. For a complete list of American consulates and embassies abroad, visit the US State Department Bureau of Consular Affairs listing on the Internet at: *http://travel.state.gov*.

Entry Requirements – Travelers entering the United States under the Visa Waiver Program (VWP) must have a machine-readable passport. Any traveler without a machine-readable passport will be required to obtain a visa before entering the US. Citizens of VWP countries are permitted to enter the US for general business or tourist purposes for a maximum of 90 days without needing a visa. Requirements for the Visa Waiver Program can be found at the Department of State's Visa Services Web site *(http://travel.state.gov)*.

All citizens of nonparticipating countries must have a visitor's visa. Upon entry, nonresident foreign visitors must present a valid passport and round-trip transportation ticket. Canadian citizens are not required to present a passport or visa, but they must present a valid picture ID and proof of citizenship. Naturalized Canadian citizens should carry their citizenship papers.

US Customs – All articles brought into the US must be declared at the time of entry. Prohibited items: plant material; firearms and ammunition (if not for sporting purposes); meat or poultry products. For information, contact the US Customs Service, 1300 Pennsylvania Ave. NW, Washington, DC 20229 *(202-354-1000; www.cbp.gov)*.

Must Know: Practical Information

Money and Currency Exchange – Visitors can exchange currency in Back Bay at **Bank of America** *(557 Boylston St.; 617-536-0712; www.bankof america.com; open Mon–Fri 9am–5pm, Sat 9am–1pm)*, and downtown at **Citizens Bank** *(28 State St. at Congress St.; 617-725-5900; www.citizensbank.com; open Mon–Fri 8:30am–5pm)*. **American Express Travel Service** has two locations downtown *(One State St., 617-723-8400; and 170 Federal St., 617-439-4400; www.americanexpress.com; open Mon–Fri 9am–5pm)*. **Travelex** is also an option, with booths at Terminals B, C and E at Logan Airport *(617-567-1087)*.

For cash transfers, **Western Union** *(800-325-6000; www.westernunion. com)* has agents throughout Boston. Banks, stores, restaurants and hotels accept travelers' checks with picture identification. To report a lost or stolen credit card: **American Express** *(800-528-4800)*; **Diners Club** *(800-234-6377)*; **MasterCard** *(800-307-7309)*; **Visa** *(800-336-8472)*.

Driving in the US – Visitors bearing valid driver's licenses issued by their country of residence are not required to obtain an International Driver's License. Drivers must carry vehicle registration and/or rental contract, and proof of automobile insurance at all times. Gasoline is sold by the gallon (1 gal=3.8 liters). Vehicles in the US are driven on the right-hand side of the road.

Electricity – Voltage in the US is 120 volts AC, 60 Hz. Foreign-made appliances may need AC adapters (available at specialty travel and electronics stores) and North American flat-blade plugs.

Taxes and Tipping – Prices displayed in Massachusetts do not include the state sales tax of 5%, which is not reimbursable. It is customary to give a small gift of money—a tip—for services rendered, to waiters (15–20% of bill), porters ($1 per bag), chamber maids ($1 per day) and cab drivers (15% of fare).

Time Zone – Boston is in the **Eastern Standard Time** (EST) zone, three hours ahead of Los Angeles and five hours behind Greenwich Mean Time.

Measurement Equivalents

Degrees Fahrenheit	95°	86°	77°	68°	59°	50°	41°	32°	23°	14°
Degrees Celsius	35°	30°	25°	20°	15°	10°	5°	0°	-5°	-10°

1 inch = 2.54 centimeters	1 foot = 30.5 centimeters
1 mile = 1.6 kilometers	1 pound = 0.45 kilograms
1 quart = 0.9 liters	1 gallon = 3.8 liters

And Toto Too

Numerous New England hotels throw down the red carpet for their VIP (Very Important Pet) guests. At the Onyx Hotel *(see Must Stay)*, **pets** are playfully greeted, given treats and adorned with a leopard-print collar tag. For an additional fee, your best friend can have his or her own bed, fleece blanket, and lunch pail full of goodies; finicky felines get their own scratching post. Fido's birthday? The Hotel Marlowe in Cambridge *(see Must Stay)* will order a cake from Polka Dog Bakery, which specializes in pet goodies. Worried about leaving your pet behind while you explore the city? You can arrange for someone on staff to visit while you're out.

Must Know: Practical Information

ACCOMMODATIONS

For a list of suggested accommodations, see Must Stay.

An area visitors' guide including a lodging directory is available (free) from the Greater Boston Convention and Visitors Bureau *(p 10)*. Check their Web site *(www.bostonusa.com)* for discount-reservation services offering the best rates in the city, and direct links to most of the hotels and B&Bs. You can make reservations online, too.

Hotel Reservation Services

Accommodations Express – 800-444-7666; www.accommodationsexpress.com.

Central Reservation Service (CRS) – 800-548-3311; www.roomconnection.net.

Quikbook – 800-789-9887; www.quikbook.com.

RMC Travel – 800-245-5738; www.rmcwebtravel.com.

Steigenburger Reservation Service – 800-223-5652; www.srs-worldhotels.com.

Turbotrip.com – 800-473-7829; www.turbotrip.com.

Hostels

A no-frills, inexpensive alternative to hotels, hostels are a great choice for budget travelers. Prices average $25–$40 per night for dorm-style rooms.

Eastern New England Council of Hostelling International – 1105 Commonwealth Ave., Kenmore Square. 617-779-0900, ext. 10. www.usahostels.org.

Hostelling International Boston – 12 Hemingway St., The Fens. 617-536-9455 or 800-909-4776 ext. 07. www.bostonhostel.com.

SPECTATOR SPORTS

With the Red Sox winning the 2004 World Series and the Patriots emerging as 2005 Super Bowl champions, Boston is a hot spot for spectator sports. The city's major professional sports teams include:

Sport/Team	Season	Venue	Phone	Web site
Baseball/ Boston Red Sox	Apr–Oct	Fenway Park	617-267-1700	www.redsox.com
Hockey/ Boston Bruins	Oct–Apr	FleetCenter	617-624-1000	www.bostonbruins.com
Football/ New England Patriots	Sept–Jan	Gillette Stadium	617-543-1776	www.patriots.com
Basketball/ Boston Celtics	Nov–Apr	FleetCenter	617-523-3030	www.celtics.com
Soccer/ New England Revolution	Apr–Oct	Gillette Stadium	877-438-7387	www.revolutionsoccer.net

BOSTON

Like the Victorian buildings reflected in skyscrapers of steel and glass, Boston is a blend of old and new. The city's role today as the administrative and financial hub of New England as well as a center of learning and culture is readily apparent. Sleek towers of commerce and government, colleges and universities, museums and concert halls greet visitors at every turn. Yet, history is the core of the Boston experience; reminders of Boston's importance as the hotbed of American independence are visible everywhere.

The Way We Were – In 1630 about 1,000 Puritans led by John Winthrop arrived on the coast of Massachusetts to establish a settlement for the **Massachusetts Bay Company**. They set their sights on the small peninsula the Indians named Shawmut and named their settlement Trimountain, for its hilly topography. Soon they renamed their new colony Boston, after the English town from which many of the Puritans hailed. Because of its maritime commerce and shipbuilding, Boston rapidly became the largest town in the British colonies.

To replenish the Crown's coffers after the costly French and Indian War, the British parliament voted to enforce high taxes and harsh trade regulations against the American colonies. This policy enraged the colonists, who, as British citizens, claimed that their rights to representation were being denied. Mounting tensions exploded into clashes between Bostonians and the British.

The **Boston Massacre** was the first of these clashes. On March 5, 1770, a group of Bostonians gathered at the State House to protest recent events. Provoked by the civilians, several Redcoats loaded their weapons and fired, killing five men.

Boston Brahmins

The "proper Bostonian," or Brahmin, descends from New England's early Puritan settlers who shared a common language and culture, and whose close-knit society set Boston apart by the 19C as the city where "the Lowells talk only to the Cabots, and the Cabots talk only to God." Stereotyped as refined, conservative and Harvard-educated, the proper Bostonian today represents an ever-decreasing percentage of the city's population.

Three years later, the **Boston Tea Party** aggravated the situation further. A tax on tea so angered colonists that in November 1773 Bostonians refused to allow the East India Company's tea-laden ships to be unloaded. Ninety Bostonians disguised as Native Americans boarded the three ships and dumped the tea into the harbor. In retaliation, England took punitive measures that served to unite the colonists even more against the Crown.

In April 1775 Gen. Thomas Gage dispatched 800 British soldiers to **Lexington** and **Concord** *(see Excursions)* to arrest Patriot leaders and seize the colonists' stash of weapons. The sexton of Old North Church *(see Landmarks)* hung two lanterns in the bell tower to signal the Redcoats' departure by boat, and **Paul Revere** made his famous midnight ride to Lexington. There, the first shots of the Revolutionary War were fired.

The Way to Be: Educated – A principal concern of the Puritans was education. The first public school in America (c.1630) and the first college in the colonies (Harvard College, 1636—now **Harvard University**) were founded in Boston. (Today there are some 68 colleges and universities in the metropolitan area.) By the 19C, Boston had become a gathering place for intellectuals and writers. Well-heeled Bostonians traveled extensively, returning home with treasures that initiated the collections of many of the museums in Boston and Cambridge.

Your visit to Beantown will no doubt include the high brow and the hip: an evening Boston symphony concert or the rollicking nightlife of an Irish pub; a historic reenactment or a performance at a cutting-edge theater. Whatever you do, you'll know you're in a vibrant city, one that reveres its past, but moves forward in a big way—think Big Dig!

Boston Fast Facts
• City population: 600,000
• Area: 48.6 square miles
• Miles of coastline: 43
• Number of college students: 250,000 (one of every 10 residents in Greater Boston)
• Number of four-year colleges in the city of Boston: 26
• Worst mistake visitors make: bringing a car into Boston proper

Neighborhoods

Boston may be small by big-city standards, but it packs a lot of personality into its compact 43 square miles. It remains a city of neighborhoods, each with its own character, style and vibe. You can go from one neighborhood to the next in short order—that's if you're not driving! Remember, in Boston it's best to walk, take the T (as the subway is called locally) or hail a cab.

Back Bay★★

It's where the fashionable shop, the trendy dine, the well-off live—and everyone watches. Built on a landfill centuries ago, Back Bay, bordered by the Charles River, the Public Garden and Huntington and Massachusetts avenues, is one of Boston's most expensive and elegant neighborhoods. Intermingled with towering churches and 20C high rises, stately rows of historic brownstones and bowfront buildings flank wide Parisian-style boulevards. Stroll the streets chock-a-block with shops, spas, galleries, restaurants, sidewalk cafes, and some of the most expensive real estate in the city.

Top Three Things to Do in Back Bay

Shop Newbury Street★★

Eight-block-long Newbury Street starts at the Ritz Carlton Hotel on Arlington Street and ends at the Virgin Megastore on Massachusetts Avenue—with scores of designer botiques, top-brand names and funky shops in between. *See Must Shop.*

Gawk at the Architecture

Along Commonwealth Avenue and Newbury, Marlborough and Beacon streets, the early residential buildings reflect contemporary French tastes—the omnipresent mansard roof and the controlled building height are dead giveaways. Post-1870s buildings west of Dartmouth Street showcase prevailing revival styles (such as Gothic, Richardsonian Romanesque and Georgian).

Go to Church

Back Bay is dotted with pretty churches, but three stand out. The 1861 **Arlington Street Church** *(Arlington St. at Boylston St.)* is famous for its 16 steeple bells—and Tiffany windows. **Trinity Church★★** *(Copley Sq.)* is recognizable by its massive central tower *(see Landmarks).* And **First Baptist Church of Boston★** *(Commonwealth Ave. at Clarendon St.)* boasts a puddingstone facade and a 176-foot-tall tower.

Touring Tip

Back Bay's east end near the Public Garden has the most upscale shops (think Brooks Brothers, Zegna, Armani, Cartier) and the area's finest residences. The farther you roam west toward Massachusetts Avenue, the less exclusive it becomes. The Kenmore Square area attracts a mixed crowd of students and young urban dwellers to its funky shops and bookstores. South of the fast-paced Boylston Street corridor, Back Bay takes on a dramatically different appearance. Here, buildings of cement and steel, such as the **Prudential Center** and **Copley Place** *(see Must Shop)* and the **Christian Science Center** *(see p 24)*, create a decidedly 20C scale and flavor.

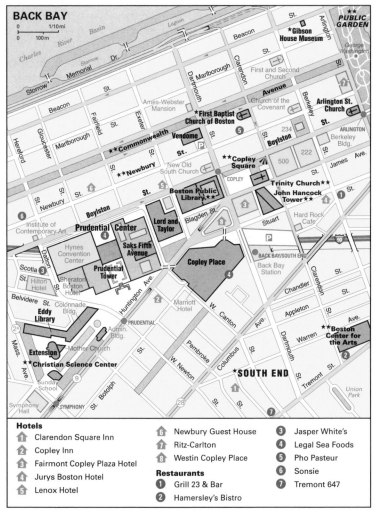

Hotels
1. Clarendon Square Inn
2. Copley Inn
3. Fairmont Copley Plaza Hotel
4. Jurys Boston Hotel
5. Lenox Hotel
6. Newbury Guest House
7. Ritz-Carlton
8. Westin Copley Place

Restaurants
1. Grill 23 & Bar
2. Hamersley's Bistro
3. Jasper White's
4. Legal Sea Foods
5. Pho Pasteur
6. Sonsie
7. Tremont 647

Neighborhoods

The Best of Back Bay

Boston Public Library★★

700 Boylston St. on Copley Sq. See Landmarks.

Christian Science Center★★

175 Huntington Ave. 617-450-3790. www.tfccs.com. Open year-round. Free tours Mon–Sat 10am–4pm (on the hour), Sun 11:30am. No tours major holidays.

This stunning ensemble of three bold concrete structures, surrounding an enormous reflecting pool (670 feet by 100 feet), houses the world headquarters of the Christian Science church. The grand **Mother Church Extension** (1906), facing Massachusetts Avenue, holds one of the 10-largest organs in the country, with over 13,000 pipes. The Romanesque-style original church (1894), with its rough granite facade and bell tower, connects to the rear of the extension.

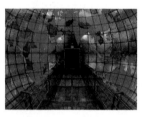

Named for the founder of Christian Science, the **Mary Baker Eddy Library for the Betterment of Humanity** opened in 2002. Step inside to experience the **Mapparium**, a 30-foot walk-through glass-paneled globe that represents the worldwide scope of the church's publishing activities. The library includes the Hall of Ideas, the Quest Gallery and The Monitor Gallery, with exhibits on *The Christian Science Monitor*, an international daily newspaper published by the church since 1908.

A New Church

A woman from New Hampshire founded Christian Science in 1866. After meditating on a Gospel account of one of Jesus' healings, **Mary Baker Eddy** (1821–1910) quickly recovered from a serious injury. After extensive study of the Bible, she felt she had discovered a science, or provable laws, behind Jesus' healing works, which still can be practiced today. She named her discovery Christian Science and wrote about this system of divine healing in her best-selling book *Science and Health with Key to the Scriptures*. In 1879 Eddy and her students established the Church of Christ Scientist, which today has branches in 80 countries worldwide.

Commonwealth Avenue★★

It's easy to imagine yourself in late-19C Paris when you see this 200-foot-wide thoroughfare. "Comm Ave.," as the locals call it, recalls the grand boulevards laid out during Napoleon III's reign; it remains a coveted address today. Lined with elm trees and punctuated with commemorative statues, this broad avenue's pleasant mall makes a good place to view a sampling of Back Bay houses on either side.

At the southwest corner of Commonwealth Avenue and Dartmouth Street, the sprawling **Vendome** (1871) was once Back Bay's most luxurious hotel; it served as a temporary home to such celebrities as Oscar Wilde, Mark Twain, Sarah Bernhardt and Ulysses S. Grant. In the 1970s it was transformed into condominiums.

Copley Square★★

Bounded by Boylston, Dartmouth and Clarendon Sts. and St. James Ave.

Named for painter John Singleton Copley *(see sidebar, below)*, this is Back Bay's main public square; it shows off some of Boston's most celebrated architectural treasures, like Trinity Church, the John Hancock Tower and the Public Library *(see Landmarks)*. Today it's hard to believe that the area was once a railroad yard.

Image Maker

Before the days of photographs, people had their portrait painted for posterity, if they could afford it. America's first important portraitist was **John Singleton Copley** (1738–1815). His paintings of well-known citizens of his day conveyed an amazingly accurate likeness of them. You can see his attention to detail in his portrait of Paul Revere in the Museum of Fine Arts, Boston *(see Museums)*.

John Hancock Tower★★ – *St. James Ave. See Landmarks.*
Public Garden★★ – *Bounded by Arlington, Boylston, Charles & Beacon Sts. See Parks and Gardens.*

South End★

See map p 23. South of Back Bay, the once-rundown, now urban-chic South End, bordered roughly by Massachusetts and Columbus avenues and Albany and East Berkeley streets (though the boundaries are a bit fuzzy), is one of Boston's hot new neighborhoods. The gentrification of this Victorian corner, with its narrow, brownstone-lined streets, parks and fountains, began in the 1980s when gays and lesbians, and artists and musicians moved in. Today you'll find a cluster of upscale restaurants, a small but lively night scene and restored town houses with million-dollar price tags. South End has attracted cultural institutions such as the **Boston Center for the Arts★★** *(539 Tremont St.; 617-426-5000; www.bcaonline.org)*, which resides in the landmark Cyclorama Building (1884). Home to artistic groups such as the Speakeasy Stage Company and the Community Music Center of Boston, the BCA offers Bostonians and visitors a full calendar of art exhibits, theater and musical and dance performances *(see Must Go: Performing Arts)*.

Beacon Hill★★

The cozy, one-square-mile enclave, bordered by Beacon Street, Bowdoin Street, Cambridge Street and Storrow Drive, shows off cobblestone streets, brick walkways, gas lamps and well maintained historic brownstones. Magnolia trees line narrow streets and window boxes overflow with flowers.

Historically the home of Boston Brahmins and the city's early black community, the Hill is the only remnant of the three peaks that made up Trimountain ridge, which once rose on the western side of the city. Its name stems from the primitive beacon that the Puritans raised on its summit in 1634 to warn of invasion by the Indians. From 1799 until the mid-19C, developers transformed the Trimountain area: Beacon Hill's summit was lowered 60 feet and the two neighboring peaks were leveled, the present street system was laid out, and the pretty enclave of English-style brick residences that we know as Beacon Hill came into being.

The south slope, between Pinckney Street and the Common, became the bastion of Boston's affluent society *(see sidebar, below)*. The north slope became the center of Boston's black community in the 19C, many of whose members worked for the well-to-do on the Hill. Today, a stroll along Beacon Hill's serene streets will transport you to a bygone era.

Beacon Hill Breakdown

Bordering the Public Garden and Boston Common *(see Parks and Gardens)*, **Beacon Street★** is lined with stately buildings, the most prominent among them being the golden-domed **State House★★** *(opposite)*. The stone and brick facade of the **Bull and Finch Pub** *(84 Beacon St.)*, popularized by the 1980s television series *Cheers*, draws TV fans for a glimpse (and maybe a pint). **Charles Street★**, Beacon Hill's commercial hub, teems with restaurants, antique shops, cafes, vegetable and fruit stands, and other neighborhood businesses.

Hobnobbing on the Hill

The "Hill" oozes Old World charm and old money. In fact, its residents, past and present, read like a Who's Who of politicians and authors: John and Abigail Adams, Daniel Webster, Henry David Thoreau, Ralph Waldo Emerson, John F. Kennedy, author Robin Cook and Senator John Kerry, 2004 presidential candidate, are a few who have lived in this exclusive neighborhood.

Massachusetts State House★★ – *24 Beacon St. See Landmarks.*

Louisburg Square★★

Mt. Vernon St. at Willow St.

This tiny residential park is Boston's most prestigious address. Laid out in 1826 on pastureland purchased from John Singleton Copley, the square now boasts multimillion-dollar restored brownstones hugging brick walkways. The Vanderbilts once lived here; today, other well-heeled Bostonions call the area around the square home *(see sidebar, p 26).*

Boston Athenaeum★

10 1/2 Beacon St. 617-227-0270. www.bostonathenaeum.org. Open year-round Mon–Fri 8:30am–5:30pm, Sat 9am–4pm.

Established in 1807, the Boston Athenaeum is one of the nation's oldest private lending libraries.

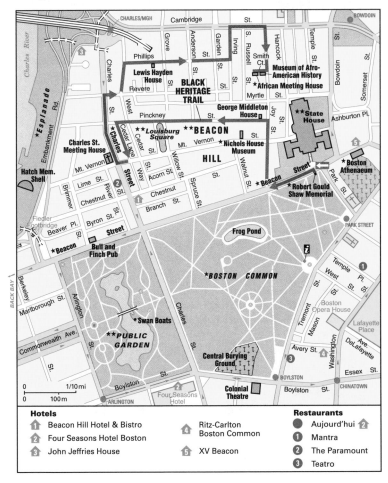

Hotels		
1 Beacon Hill Hotel & Bistro	4 Ritz-Carlton Boston Common	
2 Four Seasons Hotel Boston	5 XV Beacon	
3 John Jeffries House		

Restaurants	
● Aujourd'hui	2 Mantra
1 Mantra	2 The Paramount
3 Teatro	

North End★

North of N. Washington & Cross Sts. See map p 33.

Rooftop gardens; shops bulging with fresh meats, poultry and vegetables; and restaurants and cafes that serve home-cooked pasta, pizza, pastries and espresso crowd this colorful Italian district. Boston's oldest residential neighborhood has been continuously inhabited since 1630. Throughout the 17C and 18C, the North End reigned as Boston's principal residential district and included a community of free blacks. Irish and Jewish immigrants who settled here in the 19C eventually moved on, replaced by Southern Italian immigrants, who have maintained a strong presence.

Hanover Street★ and **Salem Street** are the main thoroughfares running through this compact, one-mile-square burg, crisscrossed by a network of narrow streets and alleyways. You can soak up the Old World atmosphere by meandering the streets, and poking into the tiny *salumerias* (delis), *pasticcerias* (pastry shops) and *macellerias* (meat markets). Then grab a seat at one of the sidewalk cafes for an espresso, and listen to the old-timers chat about their neighbors. Tourists flock over from Faneuil Hall, following the redbrick **Freedom Trail★★★** to Paul Revere's House and the North Church *(see Historic Sites)*.

The local community in the North End continues to celebrate numerous saint's days throughout the year (schedules of feasts are posted in storefronts and churches). These lively events feature religious processions, outdoor entertainment and an abundance of food sold by street vendors.

The Butcher, the Baker, the Pasta Maker

If you really want an insider's look into life and times in the North End (and a point in the right direction to the best restaurants and shops), join a **North End Market Tour** led by Michele Topor. On this two- to three-hour tour, you'll follow Topor to her favorite haunts, roaming the narrow streets and back alleys of this lively burg. She shares lots of history and personal anecdotes, sprinkled with advice on selecting the best olive oil, vinegar and pasta. You'll also meet shop owners and nibble their graciously offered samples along the way. *Six Charter St. 617-523-6032. www.micheletopor.com. Tours year-round Wed & Sat 10am–1pm & 2pm–5pm, Fri 10am–1pm & 3pm–6pm; $47.25 per person; reservations required.*

Copp's Hill Burying Ground★ – *Next to Old North Church, bordered by Hull & Charter Sts. See Historic Sites.*

North End Eateries

One of the favorite pastimes in Boston's North End? Eating, of course! If you'd like to bring home a taste of Italy, visit **Maria's Pastry Shop** *(46 Cross St.; 617-523-1196; www.northendboston.com/marias)* for home-made cannoli and melt-in-your mouth marzipan; and **Salumeria Italiana** *(151 Richmond St.; 617-523-8743; www.salumeriaitaliana.com)* for imported pastas, artisanal balsamic vinegars and other Italian spe-cialty foods. Don't miss a stop at **V. Cirace & Son, Inc.** *(173 North St.; 617-227-319; http://vcirace.com)*, a beautifully decked-out, third-generation wine store that's been in the North End since 1906. Here's a sampling of our favorite places for Italian fare:

Bricco – *241 Hanover St. 617-248-6800.* Creative, tapas-style plates are the rage at upscale Bricco. Try dishes like the grilled calamari or gnocchi stuffed with made-in-house mozzarella.

Giacomo's – *355 Hanover St. See Must Eat.*

Taranta – *210 Hanover St. 617-720-0052. www.tarantarist.com.* This small, upscale dining room serves up creative southern Italian fare with Peruvian influences. Try the grilled cotechino sausage with the Peruvian potato stew.

Pizzeria Regina – *11½ Thacher St. 617-227-0765. www.pizzeriaregina.com.* In the mood for pizza? You can't go wrong with this tiny North End eatery, which has been serving up its legendary thin-crust pizza for nearly 80 years.

The Waterfront★

Along Atlantic Ave. See map p 33.

During Boston's long period of maritime prosperity, sailing ships brimming with exotic cargoes frequented the busy harbor. Today this area is home to the **New England Aquarium**★★ *(see Musts for Kids)*, a string of waterfront prom-enades, upscale hotels, waterfront restaurants, and bustling wharves offering scenic harbor views. Constructed in the 1830s, the granite buildings on **Commercial Wharf** and **Lewis Wharf** were renovated in the 1960s into modern harborfront offices and luxury apart-ments. The original 1710 Long Wharf stretched like a monumental avenue from the Custom House Tower some 2,000 feet into the harbor to service large craft unable to anchor closer to the shore. Over the centuries its length was cut by half and its row of shops and warehouses demolished. The low-scale profile of the brick **Marriott Hotel Long Wharf** *(see Must Stay)* harmonizes well with the traditional architecture of the waterfront.

What's What along the Waterfront

New England Aquarium★★ – *Central Wharf. See Musts for Kids.*

Custom House Block

Long Wharf.

Occupying a fine site on the wharf's edge, the 1837 granite Custom House Block has been converted into a mixed-use commercial and residential complex.

Long Wharf

At the end of State St., at Atlantic Ave.

The docking point for boats offering sightseeing cruises of the harbor and its islands, Long Wharf is also the departure point for the water shuttle to the **Charlestown Navy Yard** *(see Historic Sites).*

Chinatown

See map inside front cover. Bounded by Washington, Boylston & Kneeland Sts. and the John F. Fitzgerald Expwy.

Centered on Beach Street, Boston's historic Chinatown, the third oldest in America, is rather small compared to its counterparts in New York and San Francisco. But the tiny neighborhood, squeezed in between South Station and the Boston Common, is crammed with ethnic restaurants, exotic shops and more than 6,000 residents. Enter the dragon **gateway** *(Beach & Hudson Sts.)* of this colorful, dynamic and, yes, a bit seedy enclave, and you're in a different world.

It's easy to walk in Chinatown; join the crowds and browse unusual shops and markets. At the **Vinh Kan Ginseng Co.** *(675 Washington St.; 617-338-9028)* you'll find a host of Chinese herbal concoctions guaranteed to cure whatever ails you. Supermarkets, like the **Sun Sun Co.** *(18 Oxford St.; 617-426-6494),* teem with people and exotic foods; here the aisles and counters are filled with teas and herbs, strange veggies and roots, live fish, lobsters and other sea creatures.

The best time to visit Chinatown is during one of the annual street festivals. In summer, during the first three weeks of August, there's the **August Moon Festival**; in early February, **Chinese New Year** is celebrated. Both feature dragon parades, fireworks, martial-arts demonstrations, food and dancing.

Best Dim Sum

For the best dim sum in town, grab a table at the always crowded **China Pearl** *(9 Tyler St.; 617-426-4338; www.chinapearlrestaurant.com),* where the waitstaff pushes carts brimming with choices: Peking dumplings, barbecue pork, shrimp nuggets and more. Another popular place for dim sum is **Empire Garden Restaurant**, housed in a 1940s movie theater *(690 Washington St.; 617-482-8898).*

Downtown

See map p 33. North and east of Boston Common.

Stretching from Boston Common northeast to Haymarket, downtown embraces the city's historic heart, its commercial district and the seat of city government. The renovation of **Faneuil Hall Marketplace**★★ *(see Must Shop)* in the 1970s dramatically revived the ambience of downtown by injecting new vitality into the city's center. **Downtown Crossing** *(see Must Shop)*, which was completed in the same time period, did the same; this outdoor walking mall is the focus of what is now a bustling retail district.

Faneuil Hall★★★ – *Dock Sq., main entrance facing Quincy Market. See Landmarks.*

City Hall★★

Congress & State Sts., across from Faneuil Hall. 617-635-4000. www.cityofboston.gov. Open year-round Mon–Fri 8:30am–5:30pm. Closed major holidays.

Imagine being a city council member in Boston. You would come for council meetings to this top-heavy concrete structure with a brick base. One of Boston's controversial architectural statements since its completion in 1968, the building recalls the works of architect Le Corbusier and helped to bring the so-called Brutalist style to prominence in the US. If you're architecturally minded, you'll enjoy exploring the vast public spaces on the lower floors. Oh, and you can watch a city council meeting from the fifth-floor galleries *(Wed 4pm).*

Boston Common★ – *Bordered by Boylston, Tremont, Park & Beacon Sts. See Parks and Gardens.*

Haymarket – *Blackstone St. See Must Shop.*

Union Street

When you've exhausted your shopping and eating options at Faneuil Hall Marketplace, check out Union Street. During the late 18C, this street was lined with taverns and pubs. The Duke of Orleans, who later became King Louis-Philippe of France, lived for several months on the second floor of the venerable **Union Oyster House** *(see Must Eat)*, where he gave French lessons to earn his keep. Daniel Webster was also a frequent patron here.

Historic Sites

Few places in the country can rival Boston's historical past. Home to the British government headquarters in the colonies, Boston is, after all, where the American Revolution began. It's the site of the Boston Tea Party and the Boston Massacre. It's where Patriots Paul Revere, John Hancock, James Otis and Samuel Adams are buried. There's no escaping the past in Beantown—it's pretty much everywhere!

The Freedom Trail★★★

See map, opposite. The Freedom Trail begins at the Greater Boston Convention & Visitor Center, 147 Tremont St. on Boston Common. 617-242-5642. www.thefreedomtrail.org. Visitor center open year-round Mon–Sat 8:30am–5pm, Sun 9am–5pm; closed Thanksgiving Day & Dec 25. Take the MBTA Green Line or Red Line to the Park Street T stop.

You simply must follow the redbrick road to Boston's most historic sites and attractions. A 2.5-mile redbrick or painted red line weaves through Boston's downtown streets, linking 16 historic sites.

Sites Along the Trail

The following selected sites on the Freedom Trail are organized in order as they appear on the trail, which begins at Boston Common and leads through downtown, the North End, and over the Charlestown Bridge to Charlestown.

Boston Common★ – *Bordered by Boylston, Tremont, Park & Beacon Sts. See Parks and Gardens.*

Actions Leading Up to the Revolutionary War

1764 — James Otis raises the issue of taxation without representation. Boston merchants boycott British luxury goods.

1765 — The Stamp Act is passed by the English Parliament. The Quartering Act is also passed, requiring colonists to house British troops and supply them with food. The Sons of Liberty, an underground organization opposed to the Stamp Act, is formed in many of the colonies.

1767 — The English Parliament passes the Townshend Revenue Acts, imposing a new series of taxes on the colonists.

1768 — Samuel Adams of Massachusetts writes a letter opposing taxation without representation and urges colonists to unite against the British government.

1770 — The Boston Massacre occurs on March 5.

1773 — The Tea Act takes effect. On December 16, Patriots stage the Boston Tea Party.

1775 — On the night of April 18, Paul Revere rides to warn the colonists in Lexington and Concord.

Historic Sites

Park Street Church★ – *Park & Tremont Sts. 617-523-3383. www.parkstreet.org. Open mid-Jun–Aug Tue–Sat 9:30am–3:30pm. Closed Jul 4.* Step inside this 1809 meetinghouse to see where William Lloyd Garrison delivered his first anti-slavery speech (1829), and where "America" was sung for the first time (1831).

Old Granary Burying Ground★ – *Tremont St. 617-635-4505. Open year-round daily 9am–5pm.* Buried here are Samuel Adams, Paul Revere, John Hancock and Crispus Attucks, an African American killed in the Boston Massacre.

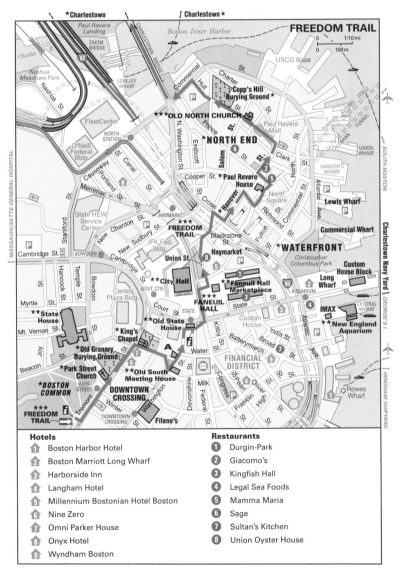

Hotels

1. Boston Harbor Hotel
2. Boston Marriott Long Wharf
3. Harborside Inn
4. Langham Hotel
5. Millennium Bostonian Hotel Boston
6. Nine Zero
7. Omni Parker House
8. Onyx Hotel
9. Wyndham Boston

Restaurants

1. Durgin-Park
2. Giacomo's
3. Kingfish Hall
4. Legal Sea Foods
5. Mamma Maria
6. Sage
7. Sultan's Kitchen
8. Union Oyster House

King's Chapel★ – *Corner of Tremont & School Sts. 617-227-2155. www.kings-chapel.org. Open Jun–Oct Mon & Thu–Sat 10am–4pm. Rest of the year Sat 10am–4pm.* Believe it or not, this 1754 granite building replaced the original wooden chapel built on the site in the 1680s. Nine years after the British evacuated Boston, this church, New England's first Anglican house of worship, was reborn as the first Unitarian church in America. Go inside to admire the striking interior, considered the finest example of Georgian church architecture in North America.

The adjoining **King's Chapel Burying Ground**★ *(617-635-4505; www.cityofboston.gov/freedomtrail; open year-round daily 9am–5pm)* is Boston's oldest cemetery, founded in 1630. This is the final resting place of John Winthrop (the Massachusetts Bay Colony's first governor), John Alden (son of Priscilla and John), and William Dawes, Paul Revere's riding mate, whom Longfellow doomed to obscurity by leaving him out of his famous poem, "The Midnight Ride of Paul Revere."

Old Corner Bookstore [**A**] *(refers to map p 33)* – *Corner of Washington & School Sts. 617-367-4004. www.historicboston.org. Open year-round Mon–Fri 9am–5:30pm, Sat 9:30am–5pm. Closed Sun.* This restored 18C brick commercial building, now operating as the Boston Globe Store, has long figured prominently in Boston's publishing world. Between 1845 and 1865, the building housed the publisher Ticknor and Fields, who published the works of such New England literati as Harriet Beecher Stowe, Henry Wadsworth Longfellow and Ralph Waldo Emerson.

Touring Tip

Don comfortable shoes, and plan on a half-day or more to walk the entire trail. You can duck into several historic sites along the way. But there are also opportunities to shop, eat and rest.

Short on time or energy? Jump off the trail when it leaves the North End, skipping the Charlestown sites altogether. Or grab a water shuttle from Long Wharf to the Charlestown Navy Yard to visit the USS *Constitution (see Musts for Kids).*

If you're on the fast track, head straight to the North End and Copp's Hill Burial Ground. From there, it's a brief walk to the Old North Church and the Paul Revere House. Or start at the Park Street T entrance at Boston Common, cross the street to Park Street Church and its Old Granary Burying Ground *(see p 33).* Then head straight to Faneuil Hall.

Old South Meeting House★★ – *310 Washington St., at Milk St. 617-482-6439. www.oldsouthmeetinghouse.org. Open Apr–Oct daily 9:30am–5pm. Nov–Mar daily 10am–4pm. Closed major holidays. $5.* Noted orators Samuel Adams and James Otis led many of the protest meetings held at Old South prior to the Revolution. The momentous rally that took place on the evening of December 16, 1773, gave rise to the Boston Tea Party. The story of the structure's history is told through interpretive displays, artifacts and recordings of passionate speeches and private conversations that are audible at various points throughout the interior.

Take a Tour

For an animated look at the Freedom Trail, join a guided tour conducted by the Freedom Trail Foundation. Professional actors and historians dress up in Colonial garb to take visitors on a whirlwind path through history. The 90-minute tour departs from the Boston Common visitor center on Tremont Street *(year-round daily 11am, noon & 1pm; $12 adults, $6 children; 617-357-8300; www.thefreedomtrail.org).*

Hand-held digital players for a two-hour **audio narration** are available from the visitor center *($15).*

Old State House★★ – *206 Washington St., at State St. 617-720-1713. www.bostonhistory.org. Open year-round daily 9am–5pm. Closed Jan 1, Thanksgiving Day & Dec 25. $5.* Boston's oldest public building (1713) was the British government headquarters in the colonies until the Revolution. In 1770 the Boston Massacre erupted on this site. On July 4, 1776, the colonies declared their independence in Philadelphia. Two weeks later, the Declaration of Independence was read from the balcony here, inciting the crowds to topple the lion and unicorn—symbols of the British Crown—perched on the structure's gables (the lion and unicorn you see are reproductions). The Massachusetts government met here until the new State House was completed in 1798. Inside, two floors feature excellent exhibits on the city, past and present. The historic balcony can be seen from the Council Chamber.

Site of the Boston Massacre

To the rear of the State House, note the circle of cobblestones embedded in the traffic island in the busy intersection of Congress and State streets, marking the actual Boston Massacre site. Five men were killed in this infamous clash between the Patriots and Redcoats on March 5, 1770. Now, look up! From this spot you'll have a dizzying look at several of the skyscrapers dwarfing the Old State House.

Faneuil Hall★★★ – *Dock Square, main entrance facing Quincy Market. See Landmarks.*

Paul Revere House★ – *19 North Square, North End. See Landmarks.*

Old North Church★★★ – *193 Salem St., North End. See Landmarks.*

Copp's Hill Burying Ground★ – *Next to Old North Church, bordered by Hull & Charter Sts. 617-536-4100. Open year-round daily dawn–dusk.* In the North End, next to Old North Church, Copp's Hill rises high above Charter Street, offering pleasant views across the water to Charlestown. The cemetery's residents include three generations of the prominent Mather family: Increase (minister and Harvard president), Cotton (clergyman and writer), and his son Samuel. The Mather plots are located in the northeast corner of the cemetery near the Charter Street gate. Also interred here are African-American abolitionist and Revolutionary soldier Prince Hall, and the remains of hundreds of black Bostonians who settled in the North End in the 18C. You can still see the bullet holes made by British riflemen, who used the gravestones for target practice.

North End Pit Stops

By the time you reach the North End along the Freedom Trail, you'll need a rest. Join the neighborhood regulars for a cup of latté at one of Hanover Street's classic Italian cafes. Try **Caffé Vittoria** *(296 Hanover St.; 617-227-7606; www.vittoriacaffe.com)*, one of the oldest in the North End, or **Caffe Paradiso** *(253 Hanover St.; 617-742-1768; www.caffeparadiso.com/Boston.htm)*.

The Freedom Trail continues across Boston Harbor in **Charlestown**★ *(see map on inside front cover).*

USS Constitution★★ – *Chelsea St., Charlestown Navy Yard, Charlestown. See Musts for Kids.*

Bunker Hill Monument – *Monument Square, Charlestown. Open year-round daily 9am–4:30pm.* Built in 1842, this soaring 221-foot-tall granite obelisk marks the spot of the infamous Battle of Bunker Hill, the first major battle of the American Revolution. The observatory, reached by a 294-step winding stairway, offers nice views of Charlestown, Boston and the harbor.

Touring Tip

Don't miss the **Bunker Hill Pavilion**, where you can watch *The Whites of Their Eyes*, one of the liveliest half-hour history lessons you're likely to encounter *(617-212-5641; www.nps.gov/bost; open year-round daily 9am–5pm; closed Jan 1, Thanksgiving Day & Dec 25)*.

Black Heritage Trail

See map p 27. Boston African American National Historic Site, 14 Beacon St. 617-742-5415. www.nps.gov/boaf. Established some 25 years ago, Boston's Black Heritage Trail winds 1.6 miles through Beacon Hill, home to the African-American community during the 18C and 19C. The trail includes 15 pre-Civil War structures and begins at the **Robert Gould Shaw Memorial**★ facing the State House. This memorial honors the leader and members of the 54th Massachusetts Regiment in the Civil War *(see sidebar, right)*.

Here are some other highlights:

African Meeting House★ – *8 Smith Court. 617-725-0022. www.afroammuseum.org. Open year-round Mon–Sat 10am–4pm. Closed Jan 1, Thanksgiving Day & Dec 25.* This handsome brick edifice is the oldest standing African-American church in the US. Built in 1806 by black Baptists for worship services, it also functioned as a forum for supporters of the antislavery movement.

Charles Street Meeting House – *Charles & Mt. Vernon Sts.* Abolitionists William Lloyd Garrison and Sojourner Truth spoke at this meeting house (c.1807). It later became an African Methodist Episcopal church, and now houses offices and shops.

George Middleton House – *5-7 Pinckney St.* Built in 1797, this house is the oldest standing wooden structure in Beacon Hill. Middleton was an early leader of the African-American community on Beacon Hill.

Lewis Hayden House – *66 Phillips St.* The residence is named for its abolitionist owner, who was a former fugitive slave. Hayden once threatened to blow the house up if anyone came looking for runaway slaves; he had two kegs of gunpowder in the basement to back up his words.

Museum of Afro-American History – *46 Joy St. (same hours as African Meeting House).* This museum is located in the former Abiel Smith School, the city's first school for black children, and features changing exhibits on African Americans in colonial New England.

The Shaw Memorial★

The Shaw Civil War Monument on Beacon Street honors Col. Robert Gould Shaw and the 54th Massachusetts Regiment, the Union's first regiment of free black volunteers. Shaw was killed in 1863 during the Union assault on Fort Wagner in South Carolina. The handsome bronze relief is the work of America's foremost 19C sculptor, Augustus Saint-Gaudens.

Go With A Guide

The Black Heritage Trail is not always easy to follow: it's not well-marked and many of the sites are private homes that can only be viewed from the outside. But don't give up on it. Use our map on p 27 (the trail is marked in blue), or go with a guide. Free two-hour tours *(Jun–Aug Tue–Sat 10am, noon & 2pm)* are offered by the National Park Service and begin at the corner of Beacon and Park streets. *For more information call 617-742-5415 or visit www.nps.gov/boaf/home.htm.*

erhaps the most iconic image of Boston is the ornate and massive Trinity Church, reflected in the mirrored glass of its sleek neighbor, the 60-story John Hancock Tower. This odd couple symbolizes the marriage of the old and new that is Boston itself. Sure, the city boasts the oldest this, that, and the other thing, but Boston's landmarks are far from stuffy. From the steeple of the Old North Church to the golden dome of the State House, these scattered gems reflect what visitors—and residents—love most about Beantown.

Faneuil Hall★★★

Dock Sq., main entrance facing Quincy Market. 617-242-5675. www.nps.gov/bost. Open year-round daily 9am–5pm. Closed Jan 1, Thanksgiving Day & Dec 25. State T stop.

This is where the action was in Boston during the years leading up to the Revolution. This revered landmark, nicknamed "the Cradle of Liberty," served as the town meeting hall, where the likes of orator Samuel Adams fired up colonists with protests against British taxes. Other noted American leaders who have addressed audiences here over the years include Susan B. Anthony, John F. Kennedy and Dr. Martin Luther King. Wealthy merchant Peter Faneuil (pronounced FAN-nul or FAN-yul) presented the building to Boston way back in 1742, but it had to be rebuilt 20 years later, after a fire caused extensive damage.

The ground floor was designed to house a marketplace like one of Olde England's country markets. Follow the staircase up to see the large meeting hall on the second floor; the big painting that dominates the front wall is George P.A. Healy's *Daniel Webster's Second Reply to Hayne*.

On the third floor you'll find historical arms, uniforms, flags and more in the **museum** of America's oldest military organization, the **Ancient and Honorable Artillery Company** *(617-227-1638; www.ahacsite.org; open year-round Mon–Fri 9am–3:30pm; closed Jan 1, Thanksgiving Day & Dec 25)*.

Can You Find the Grasshopper?

Look atop Faneuil Hall's cupola to see the grasshopper weather vane commissioned by Peter Faneuil in 1742. Modeled after the gilded bronze weather vanes that top the Royal Exchange in London, the grasshopper has symbolized the Port of Boston since the 18C. The grasshopper had special significance to Sir Thomas Gresham, who laid the first stone of the Royal Exchange. Abandoned in a field as a child, he found his way out by following the sounds of grasshoppers.

Old North Church★★★ (Christ Church)

193 Salem St. 617-523-6676. www.oldnorth.com. Open Jun–Oct daily 9am–6pm. Rest of the year daily 9am–5pm. Closed Thanksgiving Day & Dec 25 (except for services). $3 contribution requested. Haymarket T stop.

The phrase "one if by land; two if by sea" might spring to mind when you visit this famous Boston landmark. It was here on the evening of April 18, 1775—you'll recall from your childhood history lessons—that the church sexton hung two lanterns in the steeple to signal that the British had departed Boston by boat on their way to Lexington and Concord. A century later, American poet Henry Wadsworth Longfellow immortalized this church in his poem "Paul Revere's Ride." The Old North Church was built in 1723; its tall spire was twice replaced, and is now a hallowed icon of the city.

Inside the gleaming white interior you'll find handsome boxed pews, an organ and an antique clock, as well as the pulpit where President Gerald Ford initiated the celebration of the nation's bicentennial in 1976. The four wooden cherubim located near the organ were part of the bounty captured from a French ship.

Touring Tip

Step inside the combination gift shop and museum that's adjacent to the church. You might just want to purchase a replica of the famed signal lantern as a memento of your Boston trip. Or how about a pewter candle snuffer like those used in Colonial times? Historic flags, books and even tea are also for sale.

North Church Bells

Walk around the North End on a Saturday morning and you'll be treated to the ringing of the bells at Old North Church. The eight change-ringing bells, cast by Abell Rudhall in Gloucester, England in 1744, are the oldest bells in North America. The bells were restored in 1975 for the Boston Bicentennial celebration and have been rung regularly ever since. Today, they summon an active Episcopal congregation to services.

Boston Public Garden★★

Arlington & Charles Sts., Arlington T stop. See Parks and Gardens.

Boston Public Library★★

700 Boylston St., on Copley Square. 617-536-5400. www.bpl.org. Open year-round Mon–Thu 9am–9pm, Fri & Sat 9am–5pm; open Sun 1pm–5pm Oct–May only. Closed major holidays. Copley T stop.

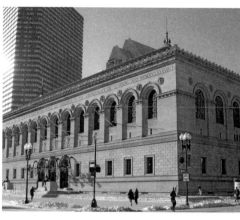

This library alone is proof that the Internet has not made libraries obsolete. Founded in 1848, the Boston Public Library (BPL) was the first in the country to lend books. It's still lending books today, plus providing free Internet access, answering millions of questions, and serving up food in its on-site cafes, among other things. The handsome Renaissance Revival-style building became the BPL's new home in 1895. Before you enter, admire the granite facade's wrought-iron lanterns, relief panels by Augustus Saint-Gaudens and bronze doors by sculptor Daniel Chester French. The inside is even more elaborate, with such features as a staircase faced in Siena marble and mural paintings by French artist Puvis de Chavannes.

Courtyard *(Accessible from ground floor)* – Pause on the landing for a peek at the peaceful courtyard, a popular lunch spot for Bostonians.

Bates Hall *(2nd floor)* – You'll know you're in the halls of learning when you enter this vast reading room. The barrel-vaulted ceiling is 50 feet high, and the long oak tables are topped with green-glass and brass lamps.

Upper Level Murals – Here you can wander through the cavernous rooms on the upper floors to admire murals by Edwin Abbey *(Quest of the Holy Grail; delivery room, 2nd floor)* and John Singer Sargent *(Judaism and Christianity; 3rd-floor corridor)*. The library's extensive Joan of Arc collection is housed in the Cheverus Room *(3rd floor)*.

Library Fun Facts

You're sure to see a title that interests you among the BPL's six-million-plus books (including those in its 26 branches). If not, there are also manuscripts, maps, musical and film scores, letters, prints, photographs and even artifacts such as handcrafted marionettes on hand. If you're a Shakespeare buff, you'll find first-edition folios by the Bard himself. There are also original music scores by Mozart and rare books from John Adams' personal library. You can read letters from celebrities like perennially "39-year-old" Jack Benny, who made radio and television audiences chuckle for years.

Fenway Park★★

4 Yawkey Way. See Musts for Fun.

John Hancock Tower★★

Enter on St. James Ave. Copley T stop.

It's a shame that the observation tower of this 60-story skyscraper is no longer open to the public. Until 2001, it was—and it provided a terrific panorama of the city. Since its completion in 1975, the Hancock Tower has reigned as New England's tallest skyscraper. Its unusual rhomboid shape creates a variety of profiles, depending on your vantage point. From the opposite side of Boylston Street, the tower, covered in 10,344 pieces of tempered glass, appears one-dimensional. From other angles it's a gigantic mirror reflecting the sky and its neighbors, Trinity Church *(see p 42)* and the old John Hancock Building (1947), identifiable by its pyramid-shaped summit topped with a weather beacon.

Touring Tip

Don't despair. You can still find places for great elevated views of the city. There are a number of sky-high dining spots that afford aerial views of Boston, especially at night *(see Musts for Fun).*

State House★★

24 Beacon St., at the corner of Park St. 617-727-3676. Open year-round Mon–Fri 10am–3:30pm. Closed Jan 1, Thanksgiving Day & Dec 25. Park St. T stop.

You can't help saying "oooh" when you first spot the golden dome of the state capitol building. The dome makes it so, well, stately. Completed in 1798 by prominent Boston architect Charles Bulfinch, the Massachusetts State House has been a cherished Beacon Hill landmark for more than two centuries. Check out the statues on the front lawn; they depict former Bostonians Anne Hutchinson, banished from the 17C colony for her religious views; Mary Dyer, hanged for her Quaker beliefs; orator Daniel Webster; and Horace Mann, a pioneer in American education.

Doric Hall – The main entrance of the building leads into this hall, named for its rows of Doric columns. Step into Nurses Hall to view paintings that immortalize such events as Paul Revere's ride and the Boston Tea Party. The Hall of Flags, lined with paintings depicting scenes from early US history, was built to house the state collection of some 400 flags, including those from the Civil War and the Vietnam War.

Third Floor Hall – Take the main staircase to the third floor hall, where you'll find Daniel Chester French's statue of Roger Wolcott, governor of Massachusetts during the Spanish-American War. This floor is where the Governor's Office is, as well as the Senate and House chambers and the Senate Reception Room.

The Sacred Cod

Peek into the House of Representatives' chamber in the State House and you'll see a strange sight. No, we're not talking about the politicians! It's the life-size wooden carving of a codfish that hangs from the ceiling. (According to city legend, the cod always points toward the ruling party.) The carving was installed in the Old State House in 1784—a gift from a wealthy merchant—and later moved to its present location to acknowledge the importance of the cod industry to the Commonwealth. In 1933 pranksters from the Harvard Lampoon "codnapped" the fish. Chamber business stopped until it was recovered, several days later.

Trinity Church★★

Copley Sq. 617-536-0944. www.trinitychurchboston.org. Open year-round Mon–Sat 8am–6pm, Sun 1pm–5pm. Copley T stop.

This imposing granite and sandstone church, completed in 1877, was responsible for popularizing an architectural style in America now known as Richardsonian Romanesque. Trinity Church is considered the masterpiece of Henry H. Richardson. The American architect studied at the École des Beaux-Arts in Paris, where he was impressed by the power and richness of Romanesque architecture. So he took this style and added personal touches to it, such as short columns and solid quoins (decorative corner blocks) on his buildings' exteriors. The massive central tower of Trinity is similar to one of the towers of the Old Cathedral in Salamanca, Spain. Step inside to see lavishly painted walls and murals and intricately carved religious scenes.

Paul Revere House★

19 North Square 617-523-2338. www.paulreverehouse.org. Open mid-Apr–Oct daily 9:30am–5:15pm. Nov–mid-Apr daily 9:30am–4:15pm. Closed Jan 1, Thanksgiving Day & Dec 25 (and Mon from Jan–Mar). $3. Haymarket T stop.

Look closely, especially if it's raining on the day you visit. The two-and-a-half-story wooden clapboard house is sometimes difficult to spot, since it's dwarfed by the taller buildings around it. Boston's oldest structure was built in 1680. It was already 90 years old when silversmith Paul Revere bought it in 1770! Revere started out on his historic ride to Lexington on April 18, 1775 from this dwelling. Inside, you'll see an account of the famous ride in Revere's own words, and Revere family furnishings, including silverware fashioned by Revere himself. Outside in the courtyard, you'll be amazed at the 900-pound bell made by Paul Revere and Sons for the **USS Constitution**★★ *(see Musts for Kids).*

Most Dubious Landmark: The Big Dig

When it was completed in 1959, Boston's elevated Central Artery carried 75,000 vehicles a day through downtown Boston. By the 21C more than 190,000 vehicles a day were traversing the roadway, creating lengthy traffic jams and an accident rate four times the national average. Today, the Central Artery/Tunnel Project is changing all that by providing an underground expressway, a new  span across the Charles River and a third tunnel under Boston Harbor.

- Big Dig construction unearthed 16 million cubic yards of dirt (541,000 truckloads) and laid 3.8 million cubic yards of concrete.
- The 10-lane Leonard P. Zakim Bunker Hill Bridge spanning the Charles River to Charlestown is the world's widest cable-stay bridge.
- Drivers using the underground Central Artery and the Ted Williams Tunnel will be monitored by more than 400 video cameras, 130 electronic message signs, 30 infrared height detectors and 6 emergency-response stations that will operate 24 hours a day.

The good news: Commuting time in traffic has decreased greatly as the project nears completion. **The bad news:** This project cost nearly $15 billion dollars, and the tunnel has sprung several hundred leaks. And so the story continues....

Museums

Once the hotbed of American independence, Boston is now a renowned center of culture, hosting world-class art and history museums. So swap the bustle of Boston's historic streets for a day or two of quiet contemplation of the city's indoor treasures, preserved within the walls of the Museum of Fine Arts and other notable institutions. The wow factor is high, for sure.

Isabella Stewart Gardner Museum★★★

280 The Fenway. 617-566-1401. www.gardnermuseum.org. Open year-round Tue–Sun 11am–5pm. Closed Thanksgiving Day & Dec 25. $10 ($11 on weekends). Museum T stop.

Prepare to be enchanted! When you step inside this treasure trove of art, you'll see a wealth of furnishings, textiles, paintings and sculpture collected by a woman who truly relished beauty, creativity and, well, life itself. Isabella Stewart Gardner *(see sidebar, opposite)* built **Fenway Court**, which resembles a 15C Venetian-style palace, to showcase her magnificent art collection. Opening onto flower gardens in a central courtyard, the galleries, permanently arranged by Mrs. Gardner herself, first welcomed the public in 1903.

Making the Most of the Museum

Ground Floor – Ceramic tiles from a 17C Mexican church cover the walls in the **Spanish Cloister**, setting off John Singer Sargent's dramatic painting *El Jaleo*.

The Courtyard – With its refreshing gardens, Venetian window frames and balconies brimming with fresh flowers, the courtyard creates an impression of perpetual summer. Classical sculptures here surround an ancient Roman mosaic pavement (2C AD) from the town of Livia.

In the **small galleries** off the courtyard, you'll find an exhibit of 19C and 20C French and American paintings, including portraits by Degas and Manet, and landscapes by Whistler, Matisse and Sargent. The Yellow Room houses *The Terrace, St. Tropez* (1904) by Henri Matisse, which depicts the artist's wife, dressed in a kimono, working on her needlepoint.

> **Touring Tip**
>
> Love flowers and formal displays? While you're at the Isabella Stewart Gardner Museum, be sure to dawdle in the flowering courtyard and the outdoor gardens. The skylit courtyard is decorated with pots and antique urns brimming with lush myrtle and bay plants; vines spill over the balconies and flowering bushes provide subtle splashes of color. Gurgling stone fountains and graceful sculpture and statuary add to the sense of serenity.

Second Floor – The **Early Italian Rooms** contain 14C and 15C works primarily from the Renaissance. The large fresco of Hercules is the only fresco by Piero della Francesca outside Italy.

The **Raphael Room** exhibits two works of the Italian painter Raphael (1483–1520): a portrait and a pietà. *The Annunciation* (attributed to Piermatteo d'Amelia) illustrates the technique of linear perspective developed in the 15C.

In the **Short Gallery**, Anders Zorn's spirited painting depicts Mrs. Gardner at her beloved haunt in Venice, the Palazzo Barbaro.

In the **Little Salon**, you'll find 18C Venetian paneling and 17C tapestries. With its 16C tapestries from France and Belgium, the **Tapestry Room** is the setting for concerts held at Fenway Court. Works by Hans Holbein, Van Dyck and Rubens grace the **Dutch Room**.

> ### Mrs. Jack
>
> Isabella Stewart, born in New York City in 1840, became a Bostonian when she married financier John ("Jack") Lowell Gardner. Daring and vivacious, Mrs. Gardner, aka "Mrs. Jack," was a free spirit whose actions were often frowned upon by other members of Boston's staid society. Art and music were her lifelong delights, and in 1899 she commissioned the construction of Fenway Court to house her fabulous art collection, part of which she gathered in Europe, and part of which was acquired in the US by her agents. Nothing in the galleries has been changed since her death in 1924.

Third Floor – Enter the **Veronese Room** to admire Spanish and Venetian tooled and painted leather wall coverings. The **Titian Room** contains one of Titian's masterpieces, painted for Philip II of Spain. In the **Long Gallery**, the life-size terra-cotta statue *Virgin Adoring the Child* provides a good example of Renaissance sculpture. *A Young Lady of Fashion*, attributed to Uccello, is characteristic of portrait art in 15C Florence, Italy.

In the **Gothic Room**, notice the full-length portrait (1888) of Mrs. Gardner painted by her friend John Singer Sargent.

Museum of Fine Arts, Boston★★★

465 Huntington Ave. 617-267-9300. www.mfa.org. Open year-round daily 10am–4:45pm (Wed–Fri until 9:45pm). Closed major holidays. $15. Museum T stop.

One of the country's leading museums, the Museum of Fine Arts, Boston (MFA) contains more than 350,000 artworks. But you don't have to see them all in one day *(see sidebar, below)*. As daunting as it may seem, the museum makes visiting easy by organizing its collections into eight departments—Art of the Americas; Art of Europe; Contemporary Art; Art of Asia, Oceania and Africa; Art of the Ancient World; Prints, Drawings and Photographs; Textiles and Fashion Arts; and Musical Instruments. Give yourself two days and see four departments per visit—or choose the areas that really interest you and concentrate on them.

Opened on July 4, 1876, the Museum of Fine Arts, Boston has expanded over the decades. But that's not the end of it. Plans are underway for a new American Wing and a doubling of exhibit space devoted to late-20C and Contemporary Art, plus other upgrades. Construction is expected to begin in 2005.

> **Touring Tip**
>
> When you buy a ticket to the museum, your paid admission allows you one free visit within 10 days. So you can return again, instead of trying to tour the entire museum in one day. Don't lose that ticket, though!

Cream of the Collections

Art of Asia, Oceania and Africa★★★ – The MFA's **Indian Art** holdings include sculpture (2C BC–5C AD), miniature paintings from the courts of North India (16C–19C), and works of jade and ivory. **Japanese Art** includes Buddhist and Shinto paintings and sculpture, scroll and screen paintings, ceramics, lacquerware, swords and woodblock prints. You'll also find an impressive group of **Chinese sculpture, painting** and calligraphy, as well as **Himalayan Art** from Nepal and Tibet. Ceramics and glass works from Iran, Iraq, Turkey and other Middle Eastern and North African countries highlight the **Islamic Art** collection. Korean Art holdings feature stoneware and lacquerware, Buddhist paintings and sculptures, and Bronze Age funerary objects. **Southeast Asian Art** focuses on stone and bronze sculpture, ceramics, and gold jewelry from Indonesia, Thailand and Vietnam.

American Paintings★★ – Prominent among the 18C portraitists represented are Gilbert Stuart and John Singleton Copley (be sure to see his 1768 portrait of Paul Revere). Works from America's 19C landscape painters include canvases by Fitz Hugh Lane, Albert Pinkham Ryder and Winslow Homer. The works of John Singer Sargent and Mary Cassatt, both of whom lived abroad, were largely inspired by European movements.

Ancient Egyptian, Nubian and Near Eastern Art★★ – The MFA's collection of Egyptian art spans 4,000 years of civilization. The sculpture of **King Mycerinus** and his queen is one of the oldest existing statues portraying a couple. Treasures from ancient Nubia (the present-day region of southern Egypt and northern Sudan) include boldly painted pottery and intricate jewelry, such as blue faience-bead necklaces (faience is a glazed ceramic made from crushed quartz or sand). Two colossal statues of the Nubian kings stand on the second floor.

Classical Art★★ – The MFA's celebrated collection includes cameos, bronzes and Greek vases; original Greek marble sculptures; and Roman sculpture in silver and marble.

European Paintings★★ – Here you'll find works from the Middle Ages to the present. Paintings of the 16C and 17C include those of El Greco and Velàzquez; the Dutch gallery boasts five Rembrandts. Bostonians' preference for the Romantics (Delacroix), realists (Courbet, Millet), the Barbizon school (Corot), Impressionists (Renoir, Monet, Degas, Van Gogh), and post-Impressionists (Gauguin) brought a distinguished group of 19C French paintings to the MFA.

Touring Tip

Pace yourself as you tour this huge museum. Take a break in one of the museum's three gardens: Fraser Garden Court, Calderwood Courtyard or Tenshin-en, "The Garden in the Heart of Heaven." And when you get hungry, you can choose among the cafeteria-style **Courtyard Café** for a quick meal *(lower level, West Wing)*; the **Galleria Café** *(first floor, West Wing)* for light fare; or **Bravo** restaurant *(second floor, West Wing)* for contemporary cuisine.

Boston Children's Museum★★ – *300 Congress St., Museum Wharf. See Musts for Kids.*

Boston Museum of Science★★ – *Rte. 28, Science Park. See Musts for Kids.*

John F. Kennedy Library and Museum★

*Columbia Point, Dorchester, near the University of Massachusetts, Boston. 877-616-4599.
www.jfklibrary.org. Open year-round daily 9am–5pm. Closed Jan 1, Thanksgiving Day &
Dec. 25. $10. JFK/Umass T stop (free shuttle bus available from T stop to museum).*

Architect I.M. Pei's sleek concrete and glass structure serves as a monument to
Boston's favorite son, John Fitzgerald Kennedy, the 35th president of the US.
Inside, you'll get to know Kennedy, the man, beginning with a film of his early
life, narrated in JFK's own words. Immerse yourself in Kennedy's 1960 presidential campaign through film footage, including excerpts from his televised
debates with Richard Nixon, and Kennedy's inaugural address. Then walk down
the re-created main corridor of the White House, where rooms on either side
hold exhibits relating to major events from Kennedy's presidency. You'll leave
the museum through the striking Pavilion, a nine-story glass-enclosed atrium
that looks out over Boston Harbor.

John Fitzgerald Kennedy

Born in Brookline, Massachusetts, John Fitzgerald Kennedy (1917–1963) grew up in a
well-to-do political family, the second of nine children born to Rose Fitzgerald and
Joseph Patrick Kennedy.

In 1936 Jack, as he was called, began his first year at Harvard University. After graduat-
ing from Harvard in June 1940, Jack joined the Navy and served in the South Pacific
during World War II. His valor in battle earned him a medal for bravery.

Encouraged by his father, JFK ran for, and won, a seat in the Massachusetts Congress in
1946; after serving three terms, he was elected to the US Senate in 1952. The following
year he married Jacqueline Bouvier, a Washington, DC reporter 12 years his junior. On
January 20, 1961, at 43 years of age, Kennedy became the youngest US president elected in US history. During his short tenure, he oversaw the founding of the Peace Corps,
the resolution of the Cuban missile crisis and the development of the US space program. His assassination in 1963 cut short the life of one of the nation's most popular
presidents, who, in the words of President George W. Bush on the 40th anniversary of
Kennedy's assassination, ". . . called our nation to high purpose, and saw America
through grave dangers with calm, discernment, and personal courage."

House Museums

Gibson House Museum★

137 Beacon St. 617-267-6338. www.thegibsonhouse.org. Open year-round Wed–Sun; guided tours at 1pm, 2pm & 3pm. Closed major holidays. $7. Arlington T stop.

Step inside this row house and you'll get a sense of the reality of 19C life in Boston. Built in 1859, the Gibson House retains its Victorian flavor and offers a rare glimpse into the lifestyle of an affluent Back Bay family. After you see the elaborate woodwork, 15-foot ceilings, imported carpets, mock leather wallpaper and plenty of curios, you'll agree that the Gibson family had both taste and the money to display it.

Nichols House Museum★

55 Mount Vernon St. 617-227-6993. www.nicholshousemuseum.org. Open May–Oct Tue–Sat noon–5pm. Rest of the year Thu–Sat noon–5pm. Closed Jan & major holidays. $5. Park St. T stop.

Don't miss this opportunity to peek inside a home with a Beacon Hill address. The Nichols House Museum is the Hill's only residence open to the public. This little brick beauty was designed by Charles Bulfinch, the architect of the State House *(see Landmarks)*, and completed in 1804. The four-story town house preserves the possessions and the colorful spirit of Rose Standish Nichols. In the spacious interior you'll see such finery as late-19C and early-20C furniture carved by Miss Nichols herself, as well as Flemish tapestries, ancestral paintings and sculptures she collected on her many trips abroad. Look for examples of her needlepoint in the bedroom.

A Remarkable Woman

Rose Standish Nichols was born in 1872. She lived during an age when women were expected to marry and have children. Miss Nichols, however, chose another path. To support herself, she worked as a landscape gardener. But her talents didn't end there; she also excelled in woodworking and needlepoint. During her long life (she died in 1960 at age 88), she was both a suffragette and a women's-rights activist. An avid pacifist, she assisted in founding the Woman's International League for Peace and Freedom in 1915.

Boston boasts the oldest public garden in America, a 34-island National Park Recreation Area, and a well-designed string of greenways and leafy malls encircling the city. When visiting, do as the locals do: take your time. Stroll the tree-lined promenades, hike the trails of a rocky island, spread a blanket in the park and smell the flowers. Here are Boston's not-to-be-missed green spaces and pretty places.

Boston Public Garden★★

Bounded by Arlington, Boylston, Charles & Beacon Sts.

This 24-acre rectangular park, bordered by a handsome cast-iron fence, was reclaimed from the swampy Back Bay in the 1830s for the purpose of creating a botanical garden. Today the popular retreat will enchant you with its flowering parterres, tree-lined footpaths and commemorative statuary

> **Touring Tip**
>
> Be sure to check out the equestrian statue of George Washington, at the Arlington Street gate. The statue, sculpted by Thomas Ball in 1878, is the first to show Washington on a horse. Follow George's gaze and you'll be looking up the perfectly aligned—and beautiful—**Commonwealth Avenue★★** *(see Neighborhoods, Back Bay).*

and fountains. Drooping willows, flowering dogwoods and fragrant cherry trees flank formal beds of roses and lilies and fiery displays of bright colored annuals. The centerpiece of the garden is the bridge that crosses the large lagoon. Here, visitors line up to board the famous foot-pedaled **swan boats**. You'll want to, too *(see Musts for Kids)*.

> ### Make Way for Ducklings
>
> *Public Garden, northeast section, Arlington T stop. See Musts for Kids.*
>
> The Public Garden is home to the cutest pieces of bronze in the city, the ducklings immortalized in Robert McCloskey's classic children's book, *Make Way for Ducklings* (1941). Combine a visit to the ducklings with a ride on the swan boats for a perfect, pint-sized piece of Boston history. For a bigger slice of same, try a Boston by Little Feet tour, geared especially for children *(see Musts for Kids)*.

Arnold Arboretum★

125 Arborway, Jamaica Plain. 617-524-1718. www.arboretum.harvard.edu. Grounds open year-round daily dawn–dusk. Visitor center open year-round Mon–Fri 9am–4pm, Sat 10am–4pm, Sun noon–4pm. Closed major holidays. Orange Line to Forest Hills station.

This 265-acre arboretum is serious stuff. It's an outdoor research/educational facility run by Harvard University and the Department of Parks and Recreation. But all you need for your visit is an appreciation for beauty and a good pair of walking shoes. Founded in 1872, the arboretum has evolved into a living museum of about 7,000 species of ornamental trees and shrubs. The place is especially beautiful in May and June when the delicate scents of blooming lilacs, azaleas, rhododendrons and magnolias fill the air.

This leafy preserve is also the final resting place of many 19C luminaries, including Henry Wadsworth Longfellow, Oliver Wendell Holmes and "Battle Hymn of the Republic" author Julia Ward Howe. Maps are available at the guardhouse.

> **Touring Tip**
>
> Try one or all of these suggested walks, which take about 15 minutes each. Ask for a map of the grounds as you enter the arboretum.
>
> - Jamaica Plain Gate to the pond area
> - Pond area to the Bonsai House
> - Bonsai House to Bussey Hill, where there's a panorama of the arboretum.

Back Bay Fens★

Fenway Park Dr. 617-635-4505. www.cityofboston.gov/parks. Open year-round daily 7:30am–dusk. Green Line E train to Museum stop.

This park is tucked behind Boston's Museum of Fine Arts—and it's like entering a different world: Part of the Olmsted-designed Emerald Necklace *(see p 53)*, the urban oasis is surrounded by highways and high rises, but inside, you'll discover a peaceful haven. It's a popular place; people come here to bird-watch (you might spot songbirds and snowy egrets), play ball on one of the fields, jog along the running circuit or tend to their gardens. The park boasts one of the oldest Victory Gardens in the country, started during World War II. Today there are hundreds of plots planted and maintained by locals. Another highlight is the pretty rose garden, enclosed by a hemlock hedge.

Boston Common★

Bordered by Boylston, Tremont, Park & Beacon Sts.

You can't miss Boston Common. Smack dab in the center of town, this public park claims a whopping 50 acres. It's a popular gathering spot for dog walkers, joggers, cart vendors, studying students and families and yes, a fair amount of homeless people. Whereas the Public Garden is quiet and contained, the adjacent Commons is open and bustling. The park has belonged to the people of Boston since the 1630s, when Reverend Blackstone sold the tract to the Puritans. Designated by these early Bostonians as "Common Field" forever reserved for public use, this landmark has served over the centuries as pastureland, military training ground, public execution site and concert venue.

- The **Central Burying Ground** (1756) fronting Boylston Street contains the unmarked grave of Gilbert Stuart, the early-American portraitist who painted the likeness of George Washington that appears on the US one-dollar bill.

Charles River Esplanade★

Near the corner of Beacon and Arlington streets, the Fiedler footbridge leads to this esplanade. Landscaped in the early 1930s, the bustling waterfront park extends more than 10 miles along the Charles River and attracts joggers, in-line skaters, cyclists, picnickers and sailing enthusiasts. If you're visiting in summertime, catch an outdoor performance at the **Hatch Memorial Shell** *(off Storrow Dr.; see Musts for Outdoor Fun)*.

Forest Hills Cemetery★

95 Forest Hills Ave., Jamaica Plain. 617-524-0128. www.foresthillscemetery.com. Open year-round daily dawn–dusk. Orange Line to Forest Hills station.

More than 150 years old, this rural cemetery garden is one of the prettiest in the country, nationally known for its collection of memorial sculpture and handsome Victorian landscape. You can stroll the 275-acre grounds, through stately groves of trees and around a small pond, enjoying scenic vistas along the way. Many prominent figures are buried at the still-active cemetery, including suffragist Lucy Stone, poets Anne Sexton and ee cummings, and playwright Eugene O'Neill.

Boston Flower Show

Just when New Englanders can barely stand the dreary winter weather, the flower show comes to town! Touted as the third-largest flower show in the world, the New England Spring Flower Show is typically held in March, filling the massive Bayside Exposition Center *(200 Mt. Vernon St.)* with over-the-top flower, landscape and garden displays. *For information, contact the Massachusetts Horticulture Society: 617-933-4900; www.masshort.org.*

Boston Harbor Islands

617-223-8666. www.bostonislands.com. Ferries, shuttle boats and tour boats operate May–Oct daily. For details about island hopping, see Musts for Fun.

Imagine a lush, nearly deserted island where you can wander, play in the surf and paddle to your heart's content. Now, imagine that same idyllic spot is a mere eight miles from a major metropolitan area. Picture that, and you've got a sense of the Boston Harbor Islands, a National Recreation Area, where nature meets man-made cityscape, separated by a splash of blue water. The area includes 34 islands, ranging in size from 214 acres to less than one acre, each with its own colorful, often bloody history, as sites of early European settlements, Revolutionary War skirmishes, Civil War forts, and prison compounds. Today they offer splendid scenery and an easy escape from the noisy city streets. Ranger-led tours, concerts, theater, children's activities and boat cruises are offered on many of the islands throughout the season.

The Emerald Necklace

Take a look at a map of Boston and you'll see a strand of green running through the city. Known as "The Emerald Necklace," this urban jewel encompasses six parks and more than 1,000 acres of public land, extending five miles from the Charles River to Dorchester. The greenway, which includes the Back Bay Fens, Riverway, Olmsted Park, Jamaica Park, Arnold Arboretum and Franklin Park, was designed by Frederick Law Olmsted, Sr., America's first landscape architect. Today Boston's Emerald Necklace is listed on the National Register of Historic Places as the only remaining intact linear park designed by Olmsted.

Boston Gets Greener

The Big Dig *(see Landmarks)* has made miles of open space available. As a result, more parks opened in 2005 than had been opened since the time of Frederick Law Olmsted. Among the new riverfront parks are North Point, Nashua Meadows and Paul Revere Landing, plus the diverse 44-mile Boston Harborwalk—from the JFK Library *(see Museums)* to the suburb of Winthrop.

There are some things so truly Boston, no visitor should miss them. That's not to say that local folk have actually done all of these, but residents do rejoice when out-of-towners come 'round so they have an excuse to experience this stuff, and to show off the city they adore.

Catch a Red Sox Game at Fenway Park★★

4 Yawkey Way. 617-267-8661. www.boston.redsox.mlb.com. Kenmore T stop.

Best Dogs in Town

Sure, Fenway hot dogs are fine if you're sitting in the bleachers watching the Sox, but when Bostonians have a real craving for dogs they hit **Joe & Nemo's** *(138 Cambridge St.; 617-720-4342; open daily 9am–9pm)*. This tiny, seven-seat diner dates back to 1909 and is still perfect for families who want a quick bite to eat, with money left in their pockets at the end of the meal. You can get a "Lil Nemo" dog for under a dollar, but adults might want to upgrade to one of the heftier links. Order them steamed, deep-fried, garlic spiced—you name it—with a choice of toppings.

Think Bostonians are prim and proper? You've never been to a Red Sox game. Or, in particular, a Red Sox–New York Yankees game, where jeers yelled out by Sox fans don't exactly bespeak couth and culture! Red Sox Fever peaked in 2004, when the Curse of the Bambino (Babe Ruth, of course) was officially reversed. That was the season the Sox, affectionately referred to as "the idiots" by teammate Johnny Damon, won the World Series after a wait of, oh, 86 years. If you plan ahead, you can still score a ticket—unless you've got your heart set on a Sox-Yankees matchup!

Built in 1912, outdoor Fenway Park is America's oldest ballpark, and home of the famed **Green Monster**, the 37-foot-high left-field wall that rises some 310 feet from home plate. You'll be as charmed as the die-hard fans, who don't want to see this piece of baseball history rebuilt. "Evvah."

Go Whale-watching

Boston Harbor Cruises depart from Long Wharf Apr–Oct. 617-227-4321. www.bostonharborcruises.com. $30. Aquarium T stop.

New England Aquarium cruises depart from Central Wharf Apr–Oct. 617-973-5277. www.neaq.org. $29. Aquarium T stop.

"Finner at four o'clock!" isn't exactly "Thar she blows!" but you'll get the idea. Seeing whales in the wild is always a thrill—and it's easy to do. A mere 12 miles out to sea from Boston lies nutrient-rich Stellwagen Bank, a 19-mile-by-6-mile underwater plateau and the centerpiece of the **Stellwagen Bank National Marine Sanctuary**. The region is a popular feeding ground for migrating whales, including humpbacks, finbacks and right

whales as well as dolphins. The whales can usually be seen in large numbers on their migration route from the Caribbean to Greenland and Newfoundland.

Cruises typically last three hours or more. Along the way, on-board naturalists point out interesting marine life and discuss the whales' feeding, breeding and migration patterns. You'll undoubtedly be wowed by what you see, as whales get near the boat and sometimes put on a real show, breaching and spyhopping as passengers "ooh" and "ahh."

Touring Tip

Bring more warm clothes on the cruise than you think you'll need (it's 20 degrees colder out in the open water), a pair of binoculars and seasick medication, if you're prone to *mal de mer* (the water gets rough out there).

Island-hop on the Boston Harbor Islands

Ferries depart from Long Wharf (parking available) or Fan Pier to George's Island. 617-223-8666. www.nps.gov/boha. New England Aquarium T-stop. For ferry information, contact Harbor Express (617-222-6999; www.harborexpress.com/harborislands), or Boston Harbor Cruises (617-227-4321 or 877-733-9425; www.bostonharborcruises.com). $10 adults, $7 children, or $25 per family.

You probably flew over the 34 little green islands that comprise the Boston Harbor Islands *(see Parks and Gardens)*, a National Recreation Area. Why not get a closer view by boat? You'll find that these islands are pleasant green places to hike, picnic, paddle a kayak, explore old ruins and enjoy dazzling views of the city.

You can even camp on a couple of the islands; the choicest spots, at the water's edge, are on Grape and Bumpkin islands *(fresh water isn't available, and everything is pack-in and pack-out; reserve in advance)*. Check out the newest island destination here, Spectacle Island, so named because its two drumlins (oval-shaped hills created from glacial debris) looked like a pair of spectacles to European settlers back in 1630. Used as a garbage dump from the 1920s until 1959, the island was rehabilitated with dirt and gravel from the Big Dig and opened to the public in 2005.

Touring Tip

If you want shell beaches, wildflower trails and campsites, go to 35-acre **Bumpkin Island**. If you want views, try **Great Brewster**, with its 100-foot bluffs and commanding lighthouse. If you want views and history to boot, **Gallops Island** is the vantage point for the city's skyline and some historic ruins. And 100-acre **Spectacle Island** has a marina, a visitor center, two beaches and five miles of trails. Take your pick!

Restaurants with a View

For dazzling overviews of the city, nothing beats a sky-high restaurant. The well-named **Top of the Hub** *(Prudential Center, 800 Boylston St.; 617-536-1775; www.selectrestaurants.com)* entices diners with innovative American cuisine and breathtaking panoramas of Boston from the 52nd floor of Prudential Center. **Intrigue**, a casually elegant eatery within the Boston Harbor Hotel *(70 Rowe's Wharf; 617-856-7744; see Must Stay)* offers lovely harbor views and global cuisine by Daniel Bruce, one of the city's top chefs. Their New Orleans-style Sunday brunch *(11am–1:30pm)* features live music. At the popular **Museum of Science**★★ *(Rte. 28, Science Park; 617-773-2500; www.mos.org)*, the 6th-floor **Skyline Room** offers awesome views of the Charles River, the Back Bay and beyond, and it's open for Sunday brunch.

More Great Views

For other excellent views of Boston, take a kayak or canoe paddle on the Charles River, or a ferry ride to the Boston Harbor Islands. Even flying in to Logan airport is a kick, as you swoop past the harbor and take in the city's skyline.

Festival Fun

There's always a festival going on in Boston, even during the dead of winter! Here are some standouts. *For details, call the citywide events hotline at 617-635-3911 or the Mayor's Office of Tourism at 617-635-4447. On the Web, visit www.bostonusa.com or www.cityofboston.gov/calendar.*

Chinese New Year – *Late January to early February*. The Chinese festival of the lunar new year brings dragonboat parades to Chinatown.

St. Patrick's Day Parade – *March 17 (parade might not be held on that date; call the phone numbers above for actual date)*. Everybody's Irish, if just for the day, and hanging out on Broadway Street in Southie (South Boston) to watch this parade.

Opening Day – *Mid-April*. Red Sox opening day marks the eternal optimism of BoSox fans (which finally paid off in 2004!).

Boston Harborfest – *Late June to early July*. 617-227-1528. www.bostonharborfest.com. In summer Harborfest commandeers Boston Harbor with a roster of waterfront activities, including the chowderfest and the annual turnaround cruise of the USS *Constitution*. The celebration ends with a bang—literally—when the Boston Pops plays a concert in **Hatch Memorial Shell** on the **Charles River Esplanade★** *(see Parks and Gardens)*, punctuated by a grand fireworks display.

Saints' Festivals – *July and August*. Italians in the North End, Boston's Little Italy, traditionally celebrate the feast days of many saints. The festivals like Saint Rocco, Saint Joseph, Madonna Della Cava and the Blessing of the Waters add color and drama to late summer—not to mention food vendors and local restaurants offering irresistible eats.

The Head of the Charles Regatta – *Late October*. 617-886-6200. www.hocr.org. Held in Cambridge, the Head of the Charles is the biggest one-day crew race in the world, and a Boston tradition, to boot.

Thanksgiving at Plimoth Plantation★★ – *Last Thursday in November. Call 508-746-1622 for details and dinner reservations. www.plimoth.org*. What better place to enjoy Thanksgiving than the place where the first Thanksgiving dinner was held—in Plymouth, Massachusetts?

First Night Boston – *December 31*. 617-542-1399. www.firstnight.org. Families have been participating in the city's alcohol-free celebration of New Year's Eve since 1976. First Night Boston features ice sculptures, a parade, fireworks and artsy activities galore. Dinner in Chinatown (a short walk away) is a must.

Musts for Outdoor Fun

Boston might not share the same outdoorsy image as Boulder, Colorado, or Bozeman, Montana, for example, but you might be surprised at the local opportunities for playing outside. The first warm days of springtime lure everyone outdoors in shorts and shirtsleeves; who cares if the wind off the Atlantic is a chill one? The best places to celebrate spring here? Sun-kissed spots include the Charles River basin, Christoper Columbus Park and the tiny, tucked-away green at Post Office Square. Here are some of our other favorite places to play.

Attend a Concert on the Esplanade

Outdoor concerts on the **Charles River Esplanade★**, the grassy area along the banks on the Boston side of the Charles River *(see Parks and Gardens)*, are a local tradition. Look for the **Hatch Memorial Shell**, a band shell, off Storrow Drive. (Parking? Well, that's another story!) The Boston Pops offers a week of free outdoor concerts in summer, including its famous, televised-around-the-planet, Fourth of July performance, complete with fireworks. The **Independence Day** festival draws upwards of a half a million people, who stake out their spot on the grass in the early morning.

Touring Tip

If you're more into music than pyrotechnics, consider showing up for the Pops' rehearsal the evening of July 3rd. Hatch Shell is also the setting for free oldies concerts, sponsored by a local radio station. These are festive, fun and Frisbee-worthy.

Beach It

Singing Beach★★

Beach St., Manchester-by-the-Sea. 29mi north of Boston. Take US-1 north to I-95 and follow I-95 north for 1.4mi to Exit 45; then take Rte. 128 northeast to Exit 16. Take Pine St. into Manchester-by-the-Sea. Limited parking. Also reachable by commuter rail from North Station, Rockport line. 978-527-2000. www.manchester.ma.us.

Set in the upscale North Shore community of Manchester-by-the-Sea, Singing Beach is easily accessible from Boston, thanks to the commuter rail. Bring your beach chair, a towel and a small cooler, but not much more in the way of gear, as you'll be walking about a mile to the beach from the train stop! It's worth it, though; this is a lovely stretch of beach, and it gets its name because it "sings" (okay, it squeaks) when you walk on it. On the way back to the train, stop at **Captain Dusty's** *(60 Beach St.; 978-526-1663)* for an ice-cream cone and enjoy it in Masconomo Park, across the street.

Revere Beach★

Revere Beach Blvd., Revere. 5.5mi northeast of Boston. Take Rte. 1A north past Logan Airport to Revere. Turn right onto Beach St. and continue to the beach. Also reachable by MBTA Blue Line Wonderland T stop. 978-535-7285. www.reverebeach.com.

More than just another sandy swatch, Revere Beach is a National Historic Landmark and America's first public ocean beach. Designed by renowned landscape architect Charles Eliot, Revere Beach has an old-time charm, thanks to its still-standing pavilions, bandstand and promenade. This is the first beach you'll encounter north of town, and it gets a colorful crowd, ranging from pre-teens in toe rings and thong bikinis to, well, grandparents in toe rings and thong bikinis!

Bike or Skate the Emerald Necklace

Unless you've got a death wish, the city streets of Boston are best left to vehicular traffic and daredevil bike couriers. A good option for cyclists is the 14-plus-mile **Dr. Paul Dudley White Bikeway**, running from the Museum of Science Bridge to Watertown. This is a multi-use trail, so etiquette dictates that cyclists stay closer to the road than the river, or risk the wrath of walkers, runners and in-line skaters. The 10.5-mile **Minuteman Commuter Bikeway** follows an old railroad track from the Alewife T (subway) station, at the end of the Red Line in North Cambridge, through the towns of Arlington, Lexington and Bedford. Don't plan to put the pedal to the metal on this one; on weekends, it's well-used by the joggers-with-babies and tots-on-training-wheels set.

Wild Blue Yonder

Just south of the city, Blue Hills Reservation boasts "wicked awesome" (in Bostonspeak) views of the city. At 635 feet, Great Blue Hill, one of nine peaks here, is the highest point on the Atlantic coast south of Maine. Okay, so it's not lofty, but it's fun to hike! The 10-mile Skyline Trail connects the nine peaks of the reservation. Shorter trails, some suitable for hiking with children, feature stone walls, sandy bogs and sun-dappled stands of hemlock and pine. Cool off at Houghtons Pond, a spring-fed kettle pond that's a favorite local swimming hole. Pick up a trail map at the reservation's headquarters at 695 Hillside Street in Milton *(617-698-1802; www.mass.gov/mdc/BLUE.htm; open year-round daily, dawn to dusk)*.

Ice Skate on Frog Pond

Boston Common. 617-635-2120. $3. Park Street T stop.

"Wintah" in Boston can be positively magical, especially at Frog Pond. When the **Boston Common★** *(see Parks and Gardens)* is dressed in twinkling lights and the ice is sufficiently solid, families and couples alike make figure eights on the ice rink here. It's a scene right out of Currier & Ives. You can rent skates *($7)*, enjoy concession treats like hot cocoa, and take a break in the warming hut.

Pack a Picnic

It's hard to imagine **Boston Common★** *(see Parks and Gardens)* as it used to be, when Bostonians grazed cattle here, and later, when British soldiers used the common as a training ground prior to the Revolutionary War. Now, this urban park—along with the **Public Garden★★**, across Charles Street—is an oasis of green in the heart of the city. In summer the Common is the setting for free open-air concerts and Shakespeare plays, while the manicured and flower-bedecked Public Garden has a more genteel feel. Find a spot on the lawn and settle in for some picnicking and people watching. Nearby places to get picnic provisions include **DeLuca's Market**, 11 Charles Street, and **Café de Paris** at 19 Arlington Street.

Paddle the Charles River

Two parking lots off Soldier's Field Rd.; look for the green-roofed kiosk. By subway, take Red Line to Harvard stop. Take #86 bus to Smith Playground and walk across the play-ground by Harvard Stadium and out to Soldier's Field Rd. Cross the street and walk 100 yards to the right. Rentals available from Charles River Canoe & Kayak. 617-965-5110. www.paddleboston.com.

Just a skipping-stone's throw from the **Boston Museum of Science★★** *(see Musts for Kids)* you'll find collegiate types muscling sleek wooden sculls along the Charles River, amid a sprinkling of sailors who skim the surface, zig-zagging like waterbugs. To become part of the picture, slip into a canoe or kayak and enjoy one of the most scenic sections of urban river in the country. Lined with parklands, the Charles River basin is part of the **Emerald Necklace** of green

space designed by Frederick Law Olmstead *(see Parks and Gardens)*. Rent a canoe or kayak, or BYOB (bring your own boat). Head upriver and glide past peaceful shores lined with willow trees; head downriver and enjoy a different view of the city, framed by arched bridges.

Wompatuck State Park

Union St., Hingham. 19mi south of Boston. Take I-93/Rte. 3 south to Exit 14; then take Rte. 228 north 5mi to Free St. Turn right and drive 1mi. 781-749-7160. www.state.ma.us/dem/parks/womp.htm. Open mid-Apr–mid-Oct dawn to dusk.

When you've had enough of city sounds and sights, there's nothing like the pine-scented woodlands of a nearby state park. This one, just 19 miles south of the city, is a favorite of cyclists, boasting 10 miles of paved paths and another 30 miles or so of unpaved, multi-use trails. These wind through lush forests and alongside fresh-water ponds, and are every bit as delightful as they sound, especially in autumn. Refill your water bottle at Mt. Blue Spring, and check out the inviting campsites; sites along the pe-rimeter road, backed by woods, are the nicest and most private. Reserve campsites in advance, or luck into one of 65 sites offered on a first-come, first-served basis.

Skiing Near the City

Sure, you could drive up to New Hampshire, Maine or Vermont to go skiing, but you don't have to. There are a couple of perfectly pleas-ant little ski hills quite close to Boston.

A family favorite is Wachusett Mountain, barely an hour northwest of the city, where there's snowmaking, day and night skiing, a high-speed detachable quad chair and 18 trails. *From Boston, take I-90 west to Exit 114A; drive north on I-495 to Exit 25. Drive north on I-290 to Worcester; turn onto I-190 and drive north to Exit 5. Take Rte. 140 north to Moore's Corners, then Rte. 62 west to Princeton. Take Mountain Rd. north to the ski area.*

Jackson Hole, it isn't, but Wachusett can't be beat for its accessible location, friendly staff and skiable trails. Wachusett State Reservation, as it's officially known, is a great place for a summer hike, too. Trails to the summit offer great views of Boston *(499 Mountain Rd., Princeton; 978-464-2300; www.wachusett.com; open for skiing late Nov–late Mar; lift tickets, $46 for adults on weekends).*

Boston loves kids, and the feeling is mutual! The city is exciting, it's easy to walk around, and it's brimming with family-friendly attractions, hands-on museums, and fun-to-visit sites. From the classic swan boats in the Boston Public Garden to the world-class Museum of Science and one-of-the-best-in-the-country Children's Museum, families will find plenty to see and do in Beantown.

Boston Children's Museum★★

Museum Wharf, 300 Congress St. 617-426-8855. www.bostonkids.org. Open year-round daily 9am–5pm, Fri 10am–9pm. Closed Thanksgiving Day & Dec 25. $9 adults, $7 children (ages 2-15), $2 children under age 2. Red Line to South Station T stop.

Honey, they shrunk the world at this bustling, multilevel museum, chock-full of please-touch fun for little tykes (best for ages 1 to 10). Kids can don helmets and strap on ropes to climb a 20-foot-high rock wall, dress up in costumes from around the world in Grandma's Attic, or step inside a two-story merchant's home from Kyoto, Japan. Children love to dig and demolish in the Construction Zone or roam through a giant two-story maze. But wait, there's more: make giant bubbles, visit Arthur the aardvark, appear in your own TV show . . . you won't do it all in one visit. Tots (ages 3 and under) have their own play area at the Smith Family Playhouse.

Touring Tip

Better block off a chunk of time for this excursion; it'll be tough getting your children to leave these fun-filled galleries. Don't miss a stop at the recycling center, heaped with interesting (and cheap!) stuff for future at-home art and science projects. Before the kids are totally worn out, visit the site's award-winning **Children's Museum Shop** for smart-kid toys, craft sets, science kits, games and more.

Puppet Show

Fairies, folk tales and fantasy rule at the **Puppet Showplace Theatre** in nearby Brookline, a short "T" ride from Boston *(32 Station St., Brookline; 617-731-6400; www.puppetshowplace.org; Green Line to Brookline Village T stop)*. This perennial favorite of Bostonian families charms young and old alike with traditional and original shows, set in the 100-seat theater. Reserve tickets ahead of time *(phone reservations only)* and arrive early for general seating. Shows for children 3 to 5 years old are held on Wednesday and Thursday at 10:30am. Weekend shows *(1pm & 3pm)* are geared to children 5 years and older *(schedules vary in summer; $8.50)*.

Boston Museum of Science★★

Rte. 28, Science Park. 617-723-2500. www.mos.org. Open year-round daily 9am–5pm (Fri until 9pm). Closed Thanksgiving Day & Dec 25. $14 adults, $11 children (ages 3-11). Combination tickets available for museum, Omni Theatre and Hayden Planetarium. Green Line to Science Park T stop.

More than 600 interactive exhibits, a planetarium and observatory, and a theater with a five-story screen greet you when you visit this highly regarded museum along the Charles River. Here children can explore science and technology through cutting-edge, hands-on exhibits. Push-button displays and life-size models make it easy to participate in such activities as playing with lightning produced by a Van de Graaff generator or "flying" through the cosmos in models of American spacecraft. You can also watch new chicks hatch, peer through the world's largest magnifying glass, and gaze at galaxies and quasars at the **Charles Hayden Planetarium**.

Boston Public Garden★★ for Kids

Bounded by Arlington, Boylston, Charles & Beacon Sts. Green Line to Arlington T stop. See Parks and Gardens.

Sure, this popular city oasis is pretty, but who cares if you're a kid? The star attraction for families is the famous **swan boats**, an enduring symbol of Boston. These pedal-powered boats have been delighting visitors and locals since 1877. As the oh-so-slow watercraft move across the Public Garden Lagoon, friendly ducks trail along looking for handouts. This is the setting for Robert McCloskey's book *Make Way for Ducklings*, the classic children's story of a mallard family looking for a home. After the ride, search for the bronze replicas of the story's characters in the park; it's a popular place for a family photo. *Swan boats depart from the pavilion in the center of the garden (mid-Apr–mid-Sept daily 10am–4pm; $2.50 adults, $1 children ages 2-15; 617-522-2966; www.swanboats.com).*

Splish-splashing in Frog Pond

The 440-foot-long spray pool at Frog Pond on Boston Common *(see Parks and Gardens)* is a great place for a summer cool-down. The shallow water, just 6 to 18 inches deep, makes a fine wading spot for little ones; older kids love to stand under the bubbling fountain. Lifeguards are on duty, concessions are nearby, and picnic tables have umbrellas. Even swim diapers (required for toddlers) are available at the concession stand. Come winter, Frog Pond is a favorite spot for ice-skating *(see Musts for Outdoor Fun)*.

New England Aquarium★★

Central Wharf, off Atlantic Ave. (adjacent to the Marriott Hotel). 617-973-5200. www.neaq.org. Open year-round Mon–Fri 9am–5pm, weekends 9am–6pm. Closed Thanksgiving Day & Dec 25. Aquarium: $15.95 adults, $8.95 children (ages 3-11). IMAX: $8.95 adults, $6.95 children. Combination tickets are available for Aquarium & IMAX: Blue Line to Aquarium T stop.

Perched on Boston's pretty waterfront, this four-story, glass and stainless-steel spiral aquarium is one of the city's most beloved attractions. Where else can you see fish with glow-in-the-dark eyeballs, rare Australian sea dragons, 12-foot-long moray eels, and fish that change their colors? In all, the aquarium is home to more than 8,000 fish, invertebrates, mammals, birds, reptiles and amphibians found around the world.

The towering cylindrical **ocean tank**, in the center of the aquarium, contains a re-creation of a Caribbean coral reef, chock-full of coral and sponges. Circle the 200,000-gallon saltwater tank to watch sharks, sea turtles, moray eels and hundreds of species of fish swim within inches of your face. Be sure to look for Myrtle, the 45-year-old (and counting) resident green sea turtle.

Kids flock to the **Edge of the Sea** tide pool to dunk their hands in the water and grab hold of crabs, sea stars and urchins. At the penguin exhibit *(ground floor)*, you'll see African penguins from South Africa and Namibia, rockhoppers from South America and little blue penguins from Australia and New Zealand, frolicking on the rocks and slipping in and out of the chilled (and filtered!) Boston Harbor water. And everyone loves the harbor seals that play in the outdoor tank, entertaining lunchtime crowds and passersby.

IMAX – Adjacent to the aquarium is the massive, six-story-high IMAX theater, showing science and conservation-themed movies, like *Into the Deep, Volcanoes of the Deep Sea* and *Ocean Wonderland 3D*.

Touring Tip

The aquarium also offers whale-watching cruises where naturalists provide running commentary—and sightings are guaranteed *(trips offered mid-Apr–Oct; for information and reservations, call 617-973-5200 or visit www.neaq.org; for more on whale-watching excursions, see Musts for Fun).*

USS Constitution★★

Boston National Historical Park, Charlestown Navy Yard, Charlestown. 617-426-1812. www.ussconstitutionmuseum.org. Ship open Nov—early Apr Thu—Sun 10am—3:50pm; rest of the year Tue—Sun 10am—3:50pm. Museum open May—mid-Oct daily 9am—6pm; rest of the year daily 10am—5pm. Both closed Jan 1, Thanksgiving Day & Dec 25. Water shuttle from Long Wharf, or Green or Orange Lines to North Station.

Do you know how the USS *Constitution* got its nickname, "Old Ironsides"? It's said that cannonballs were seen bouncing off her oak sides during the War of 1812. You'll learn that and much more on a tour of this famous ship. Undefeated in battle, Old Ironsides was originally launched in Boston in 1797, making it the oldest commissioned warship afloat in the world. Climb aboard for a tour, led by an active-duty sailor. You'll poke around the old ship's nooks and crannies, and get an idea of life onboard.

> **The Ships Have Come In**
>
> A spanking new and expanded version of the popular **Boston Tea Party Ship & Museum** is due to open in late 2005 *(Congress St. Bridge; Red Line to South Station)*. The lively, costumed presentations at the museum celebrate and relive the infamous December 16, 1773 Boston Tea Party event that sparked the American Revolution. Two new tea party replica ships will be brought in, and the museum's replica of the original brig, *Beaver II*, has been completely overhauled. *For updates, call 617-269-7150 or visit www.bostonteapartyship.com.*

Kids will like the adjacent **USS Constitution Museum** even better. Here, they can hoist a sail, fight a (video) battle with the British, fire a cannon and play captain of a ship at a computer simulator. On-site artisans demonstrate traditional maritime crafts, like knot tying and model shipbuilding.

> ### Ranger Tours
>
> Boston Park rangers offer great programs for children throughout the year. Families can join the rangers on guided nature programs that might include a hunt for urban animals or a visit to a pond to search for freshwater critters. Favorites include the stable tour, where kids can meet some of the horses in Boston's mounted ranger unit; and a reading of Robert McCloskey's *Make Way for Ducklings* in Boston's Public Garden. *For information, contact the Department of Parks and Recreation (1010 Massachusetts Ave.; 617-635-7487; www.cityofboston.gov/parks).*

Tours of Fenway Park★★

4 Yawkey Way. 617-226-6666. www.redsox.com. Tours depart from the souvenir store across Yawkey Way year-round daily 9am–4pm (on the hour) or until three hours before game time, whichever is earlier. $12 adults, $10 children (ages 14 and under). Green Line to Kenmore T stop. For information on game tickets, see Musts for Fun.

Baseball aficionados and aspiring batters, here's your chance to go behind the scenes at the much-revered Fenway Park, the oldest field in Major League Baseball. The intimate home of the 2004 World Series Champion Boston Red Sox hasn't changed much since the day it opened on April 20, 1912. You'll touch the famous **Green Monster** left-field wall (did you know that it's 37 feet tall?), visit the press box, get your photo taken by the dugout, and take a seat in the private club overlooking the field. The tour also includes a stroll around the field, and a visit to the impressive Red Sox Hall of Fame—a premium, glassed-in seating area filled with memorabilia, photos and plaques honoring Red Sox Hall of Famers. Fenway was home to

baseball greats Babe Ruth, Bobby Doerr, Cy Young, Ted Williams, Carlton Fisk and Carl Yastrzemski, among others. Of course, your kids are more likely to think of Pedro Martinez, David Ortiz and Manny Ramirez, the boys of summer 2004.

The Longest Home Run

You'll learn lots of fun tidbits on the tour (did you know that no player has ever hit a home run over the right-field roof at Fenway Park?). Before you leave the park, take a look into the right-field bleachers. The seat painted red marks the landing spot of the longest measurable home run hit inside Fenway Park. Ted Williams hit the home run on June 9, 1946 off Fred Hutchinson of the Detroit Tigers. The blast was measured at 502 feet. Legend says that the ball crashed through the straw hat of the man sitting in the seat—section 42, row 37, seat 21.

Fenway's Features

- **The Bullpen** – This is where the pitchers warm up before and during a game. The coach uses the red phone in the bullpen to call for relief pitchers.
- **The Dugout** – Ball players sit here during the game. It's right at the level of the field.
- **The Green Monster** – This plastic-covered metal wall was colored green to be less distracting for the hitters.
- **Pesky's Pole** – The foul pole is 302 from home plate. Johnny Pesky, who played for the Red Sox from 1942 to 1954, batted balls off it or around it, for home runs.
- **Press Box** – News reporters sit in this glass-enclosed space to watch the game and write about it. The glass is unbreakable, so the people in the press box don't get hit by baseballs (balls hit the glass more often than you'd think).

Boston By Little Feet

Tours start in front of Faneuil Hall (Congress St. side), May–Oct Sat & Mon 10am, Sun 2pm. 617-367-2345. www.bostonbyfoot.com. $8. Blue line to Aquarium/Faneuil Hall, Green Line to Government Center or Orange Line to State St. T stop.

History class was never so much fun! This hour-long walking tour is the perfect kid-friendly introduction to Beantown. Designed for children ages 6 through 12, the guided tour covers a major portion of the **Freedom Trail★★★** *(see Historic Sites)*. Kids get a special explorer's map with footprints leading to major locations on the tour with lots of opportunity for participation and zany antics. Families with children of all ages may also enjoy the Bells, Bridges & Locks tour. On this hour-long walk, you'll poke around and under the water behind the North Station and FleetCenter. Note: Children must be accompanied by an adult.

> **A Quick Bite**
>
> Hungry families can't go wrong at **Quincy Market** in **Faneuil Hall Marketplace★★** *(617-242-5642; www.faneuilhallmarketplace.com; see Must Shop)*. It's the perfect grazing spot, with tons of food stalls and pushcart vendors offering nearly every imaginable food-stuff. Let everyone pick what they want, then meet at a table in the center courtyard or at an outside bench. Expect crowds; this place is jumpin' all the time.

Festival Fun for Kids

What kid doesn't like a party? Family-friendly Boston sponsors a host of events that are geared toward children. Grab your parents and come on down!

Duckling Day Parade – *May. 617-426-1885*. Dress as your favorite character from the children's classic *Make Way for Ducklings* and join the fun. The parade is held on Boston Common *(bounded by Beacon, Boylston, Tremont & Park Sts.)* on Mother's Day.

Franklin Park Kite & Flight Festival – *Mid- to late May. 617-635-4032*. Go fly a kite at this festival, which features kite making, music and family fun. Held at Franklin Park Golf Course *(1 Franklin Park Rd., in Dorchester)*.

Harborfest Children's Day – *Late June. 617-227-1528. www.bostonharborfest.com*. Part of the city's popular Harborfest, this special day for kids features balloons, face painting, educational activities and more. It's held at City Hall Plaza *(Congress St.)* in downtown Boston.

A thriving rock scene (thanks to the influx of thousands of college students), a revived theater district and a centuries-old reverence for classical music make Boston a hotbed for performing arts. From tiny jazz clubs to megamusic tours, from Boston Pops concerts to performances by new artists, you'll find something to do nearly every night of the week.

Boston Symphony Orchestra★★★

Symphony Hall, 301 Massachusetts Ave. 617-266-1200. www.bso.org. Green Line to Symphony T stop or Orange Line to Massachusetts Ave. T stop.

Since 1881 this highly-acclaimed orchestra has been entertaining Boston audiences. Today the renowned Boston Symphony Orchestra (BSO) performs in the historic 2,625-seat Symphony Hall, which opened in 1900 and remains one of the world's finest performing-arts spaces. For nearly 20 years, the BSO held its concerts in the Old Boston Music Hall (1852); now named the Orpheum Theater, the venue continues to host musical events. Generally, the orchestra performs in Symphony Hall from October through April.

Boston Pops★★

Symphony Hall, 301 Massachusetts Ave. 617-266-1200. www.bso.org. Green Line to Symphony T stop or Orange Line to Massachusetts Ave. T stop.

In May and June, and during the Christmas holidays, Symphony Hall's outstanding acoustics reverberate with the sounds of the Boston Pops. The idea for the Boston Orchestra's performances of "lighter music" became a reality in 1885, when the first Promenade concert was held (Promenade was the original name of the Pops). In 1974 the orchestra began its annual Fourth of July celebration and Christmas holiday concerts. The Boston Pops' tradition of a week of free outdoor shows in summer, culminating in its famous Fourth of July concert with fireworks, continues at the Hatch Shell on the Charles River Esplanade. Throw down a blanket and join the crowds.

Touring Tip

If you're looking for a bargain, join the rush ticket line at Symphony Hall the day of a Boston Symphony Orchestra performance. A limited number of $8, same-day tickets are available for Tuesday and Thursday evenings and Friday afternoons *(one per customer; cash only)*. Boston Pops also offers discounted same-day tickets *($10)* for Tuesday night performances during its spring-summer season. Can't make those nights? Attend an open rehearsal at $16 a ticket. *For more information, call 617-266-1200 or check online at www.bso.org.*

Boston Center for the Arts★★

*539 Tremont St., between Berkeley & Clarendon Sts. 617-426-2787. www.bcaonline.org.
Box office open Wed–Sat noon–5pm. Green Line to Copley Square T stop or Orange Line
to Back Bay T stop.*

If you're looking for some cutting-edge theater and art, this one-stop center is the place to go. The four-acre complex includes resident companies the Pilgrim Theater, the Speakeasy Stage Company, the Súgán Theatre Company and the Theater Offensive, known for their contemporary—and often daring—plays and performances. Hosting more than 45 productions each year, the center is considered one of the best venues in Boston for small-theater offerings.

The 23,000-square-foot **Cyclorama**, an 1884 building on the National Register of Historic Places, is home to an array of changing exhibits and performances showcasing contemporary works by established and emerging artists. It also houses the Community Music Center of Boston, the Art Connection, the Boston Ballet Costume Shop, three small theaters and a rehearsal studio. Originally an organ factory built in 1850, the Tremont Estates Building now encompasses more than 50 artists' studios, as well as the 2,200-square-foot **Mills Gallery**, where the BCA stages about six large-scale exhibits a year *(open year-round Wed–Thu & Sun noon–5pm, Fri–Sat noon–10pm)*. The added benefit is that you'll have lots of opportunities to engage with artists through artist's talks, curator's talks and other related events.

Here's What's Happening

The Thursday Calendar section and Sunday Arts section of the *Boston Globe* have extensive entertainment listings for the city and surrounding suburbs. The hipper, more avant-garde *Boston Phoenix*, published on Thursdays, also has a good rundown of events and performances, including some of the more off-the-wall happenings.

Cheap Tickets

On a budget? Head to one of the **BosTix** kiosks at Faneuil Hall *(617-482-2849; www.artsboston.org/bostix.cfm; Tue–Sat 10am–6pm, Sun 11am–4pm)* and at Copley Square near Boylston and Dartmouth streets *(Mon–Sat 10am–6pm, Sun 11am–4pm)*. Get there early and you're likely to snag same-day, half-price, cash-only tickets to some of the city's top performances of music, theater, dance and opera. BosTix also has information about, and advance tickets for other events, including sports.

American Repertory Theatre

Loeb Drama Center, 64 Brattle St., Cambridge. 617-547-8300. www.amrep.org. Box office open Tue–Sun noon–5pm. Red Line to Harvard Square T stop.

This award-winning group, under the artistic direction of Robert Woodruff, is one of the country's most acclaimed resident theater companies. Located at the Loeb Drama Center on Harvard Square in Cambridge, the company presents a mix of drama, music, comedy, classics and new works.

> **Touring Tip**
>
> Parents with kids in tow should check out the child-care program offered during Saturday matinees at the American Repertory Theatre.

Berklee Performance Center

136 Massachusetts Ave. 617-747-2261. www.berkleebpc.com. Box office open Mon–Sat 10am–6pm, and 2 hours prior to show time on performance days. Green Line to Hynes Convention Center T stop.

Here's the place to hear jazz, funk, soul, gospel, Celtic, Latin and more at wallet-pleasing prices: $5 to $10 for most events. The 1,220-seat hall, part of the Berklee College of Music, is known for performances of music from around the world throughout the year, as well as by the college's top talent.

Colonial Theatre

106 Boylston St. 617-426-9366. www.broadwayinboston.com. Box office open non-performance days: Mon–Sat 10am–6pm; performance days: Tue–Sat 10am & Sun noon, until a half hour after curtain time; Sun matinees: noon-6pm. Green Line to Boylston St. T stop or Red Line to Chinatown T stop.

Come to this historic playhouse just to see its lavishly restored plasterwork, intricate murals, vivid stenciling and shimmering gold leaf. The city's oldest continuously operating theater has faced Boston Common for nearly 10 decades. Today the 1,700-seat hall is a popular venue for pre-Broadway tryouts.

Jordan Hall

30 Gainsborough St. 617-536-2412. www.newenglandconservatory.edu. Box office open Mon–Thu noon–6pm, Fri 10am–3pm, weekends two hours before performance. Green Line E train to Symphony T stop or Orange Line to Massachusetts Ave. T stop.

One of America's finest concert venues, Jordan Hall has nearly perfect acoustics. The historic 1,013-seat building (1903) serves as the performance hall for the **New England Conservatory**, an internationally recognized music conservatory which uses the plush hall for lectures, seminars and some 450 free classical, jazz and improvisational music concerts a year.

The hall is also home to the **Boston Philharmonic** *(617-236-0999; www.bostonphil.org)*, conducted by Benjamin Zander. Don't miss one of Zander's pre-concert lectures *(Sat at 6:45pm)*, which include his personal insights into the music. The Boston Philharmonic also performs on Sunday afternoons at the Sanders Theatre at Harvard University *(Memorial Hall, 45 Quincy St.; 617-496-2222)*. The pre-concert lecture for the Sanders Theatre Series (Sunday afternoons) begins at 1:45pm.

Shubert Theatre

265 Tremont St. 617-482-9393. www.wangcenter.org. Box office open Mon–Sat 10am–6pm. Green Line to Boylston St. T stop or Red Line to Park St. T stop.

This intimate turn-of-the-20C theater is home to Boston's Lyric Opera company. The playhouse also hosts a variety of classical plays, and a popular family series, including shows like *A Year With Frog and the Toad* and *The Little Prince*.

Wang Center

270 Tremont St. 617-482-9393. www.wangcenter.org. Box office open Mon–Sat 10am–6pm. Green Line to Boylston St. T stop or Red Line to Park St. T stop.

A prominent landmark in Boston's historic theater district, the opulent Wang Center underwent a massive $9.8 million restoration in the early 1990s. Today the 1925 building, which looks like one of Louis XIV's palaces, glitters with chandeliers and imported marble. The Wang is one of only a handful of theaters around the world that can accommodate large, complicated productions such as musicals *Les Miserables* and *The Phantom of the Opera* and performances such as *Riverdance–The Show*. The center is also home to the nationally acclaimed **Boston Ballet** *(617-695-6955; www.bostonballet.org)*.

Must Shop

Boston's retail scene appeals to many tastes. Thrifty Yankees, well-heeled international students with platinum credit cards, Brahmin snobs and Cambridge beads-and-Birks types all have their shopping haunts. Sometimes, they even overlap; Newbury Street, for example, has everything from Cartier to comic books. Not up on the latest and hippest? Not to worry. By the time the retail world has caught on to the Next Big Thing, the area's 200,000-plus college students will have long abandoned it!

Touring Tip: Orient Yourself

Back Bay's eight-block-long Newbury Street starts at the Ritz Carlton Hotel on Arlington Street and ends at the Virgin Megastore on Massachusetts Avenue—with designer boutiques, top brand names and funky shops in between. **Boylston Street**, one block over, is another shopping stronghold. Prefer a mall setting and big-name stores? Check out **Copley Place**, a high-end mall anchored by Neiman Marcus. Next door, you'll find Saks Fifth Avenue and more than 75 shops and eateries within **Prudential Center**.

Faneuil Hall Marketplace★★

State St. at Congress St. 617-523-1399. www.faneuilhallmarketplace.com. Open year-round Mon–Sat 10am–9pm, Sun noon–6pm. Haymarket T stop.

A shell's toss from Union Oyster House *(see Must Eat)*, this urban marketplace is also known as **Quincy Market**, for the long Greek Revival-style arcade that serves as the centerpiece of the complex. In total, three restored granite buildings constructed in 1825 house 50 shops, 14 full-service restaurants and 40-some food stalls. The place is more of a draw for its ambience than its retail mix. The complex attracts hordes of tourists who might well find the same shops, like Ann Taylor and Sunglass Hut, in their own local malls. But there's a buzz here, created by the presence of jugglers, musicians and street performers. You may even spot a Benjamin Franklin look-alike. Fun photo op: Pose a loved one next to the bronze of a cigar-chompin' Red Auerbach, legendary coach of the Boston Celtics from 1950 to 1966.

Touring Tip

Skip the retailers lining the north and south marketplace buildings, and proceed directly to Quincy Market. The food stalls set chock-a-block here make for great grazing. Get your "chowdah" here, your pizza there and a big, gooey Boston baked brownie over yonder . . . though most Bostonians would be loathe to admit it, this touristy haunt is a great place to go for Sunday brunch.

Newbury Street★★

Between Commonwealth Ave. & Boylston Sts., Back Bay. www.newbury-st.com. Arlington, Copley or Boylston T stops.

Dress the part if you plan to shop here—Boston's most upscale shopping drag is the city's answer to New York's Fifth Avenue. A picture-perfect retail row lined with spiffy town houses, Newbury Street boasts a happy sprinkling of boutiques, restaurants, ice-cream shops and sidewalk cafes. Set in Back Bay, the street is easy to navigate: cross streets are lettered from A (Arlington) to H (Hereford). In between, you'll find designer shops oozing with attitude, like **Gianni Versace** *(no. 12)* and **Ermenegildo Zegna** *(no. 39)*, and kickier duds at shops like **Jasmine Sola** *(no. 329)*, **Sola Men** *(no. 344)* and **Betsey Johnson** *(no. 201)*. For funkier finds, like sequined '70s rock-band tees and trashy tank tops, there's **Urban Outfitters** *(no. 361)* and **Allston Beat** *(no. 348)*. For those with grown-up tastes and the cash to afford them, Newbury Street offers plenty of places to lay those Benjamins down, including **Cartier** *(no. 40)*, **Burberry** *(no. 2)* and **Chanel Boutique** *(no. 5)*.

> **Best Thing about Newbury Street**
>
> Art galleries and tiny specialty shops, like **Fresh** *(no. 121)* for cosmetics, and **Kitchen Arts** *(no. 161)*, are nestled alongside ice-cream shops.

Copley Place

Two Copley Pl. 617-262-6600. www.simon.com. Copley T stop. Connects to Prudential Center via the skywalk.

Located behind the Boston Public Library, Copley Place is the only mall in Boston proper. And a swank one it is, with rosy marble and polished brass. High-end retailers like **Gucci** and **Tiffany** reside here, along with anchor **Neiman Marcus**—more than 100 in all. Less familiar names are sprinkled among the biggies. Some to seek out: **The Artful Hand Gallery**, representing some 500 artisans; **Thomas Pink**, for tailored classic shirts; and **be jeweled**, featuring an array of sparkly hair clips and antique jewelry.

> **Touring Tip**
>
> Post-shopping, settle in for chowder at **Turner Fisheries** (winner of the Boston Chowderfest for so many years, they've retired from the competition) and a matinee at the Copley Place multiplex.

Downtown Crossing

Intersection of Washington, Winter & Summer Sts. 617-482-2139.
www.downtowncrossing.org. Downtown Crossing T stop.

This lively pedestrian mall, tucked behind Boston Common, is a colorful retail mishmash of big department stores, pushcart vendors and diamond merchants. Madly in love? Spring for some bling at the **Diamond Exchange**. Dozens of jewelers call Downtown Crossing home. Madly in love . . . with shoes? Face temptation at **DSW Shoes** and **Skechers USA**, among others. Downtown Crossing is a favorite haunt of bargain hunters, too, thanks to discount stores like **H&M**, **Marshall's**, **Eddie Bauer Outlet** and **T.J. Maxx**. Of course, a big draw here is the diva of discounters, **Filene's Basement** *(below)*.

Filene's

426 Washington St., at Downtown Crossing. 617-357-2100. Downtown Crossing T stop.

If there's anyplace to shop that is totally Boston, it's Filene's. Founded in 1881 by William Filene, the department store sits within a Beaux-Arts building that features six floors of merchandise, from infantwear to housewares, clothing to cosmetics. In 1908 Filene's son Edward had a brainstorm—if merchandise hadn't sold within a predetermined period of time, it would be moved to the store's basement and marked down in progressive stages: 25% after two weeks, 50% after three weeks, and 75% after one month. Unsold items would be donated to charity. Over the years, **Filene's Basement** has become a virtual institution in the northeast. Although it's no longer owned by the Filene Company, Filene's Basement still occupies the lower level of the flagship store. The Basement, as it's known, is the oldest off-price store in the US and is still unbeatable when it comes to uptown duds at downtown prices.

> **Touring Tip**
>
> Avoid the other Filene's Basement satellite stores and do your digging at this one, where stock from Barney's, Bergdorf Goodman and other posh stores comes for one last shot at a good home! Every Boston shopaholic has a tale of an Ultimate Find at the Basement— true Yankees like to boast about how little they paid for something.

Haymarket

Bordering Blackstone St., just north of Faneuil Hall Marketplace.

Say what you will about homogenized, one-size-fits-all American shopping, but real shopping—as in haggling, shouting, pushing and shoving—is not dead yet. Boston has the Haymarket, a colorful outdoor marketplace of fish sellers and purveyors of fresh flowers and produce. Located near Faneuil Hall Marketplace, and a hop and a skip from the North End—Boston's "Little Italy"—the Haymarket is a Friday-and-Saturday-only shopping event. Assertive vendors offer "a bagga oranges, only a dollah!" and other bargains that get better as the day progresses. Like many a good marketplace, there's no official opening or closing time, although the action generally starts around 6:30am (best time to find parking in the 'hood as well) and goes until everything is gone. The produce is better earlier (vendors will yell at you if you pick and choose—this is strictly "'grab-and-go' shopping!), but the prices are cheaper later. Then again, moods worsen, so you're on your own here. Watch out for the super salesfolk—they're so good, you may well end up heading home with a bag full of eels, or other impulse items.

The Shops at Prudential Center

800 Boylston St. 617-236-3100 or 800-746-7778. www.prudentialcenter.com. Copley T stop. Connects to Copley Place via the skywalk.

The towering 52-story "Pru" is one of Boston's best-known landmarks, combining office, residential and retail space. During Boston's interminable winter, Prudential Center is a "two-fer" shopping zone, since the Pru is a short-but-labyrinthian indoor walk from Copley Place. Among the 75-plus shops and restaurants are the region's only **Saks Fifth Avenue**, **Lord & Taylor** and Boston's largest **Barnes & Noble** bookstore. Most of these stores—The Body Shop, Ann Taylor—you've seen before, but the eats are above par, including **California Pizza Kitchen** and **Legal Sea Foods**. The coolest shop here is the boho-chic **Anthropologie**, sitting across the street at 799 Boylston.

Baubles and Bijoux

Keep your Tiffany's and your Cartier. Proper Bostonians tend to buy their baubles and bling bling at **Shreve, Crump & Low** (300 Boylston St.; 617-267-9100; *www.shrevecrumpandlow.com*), America's oldest jewelry store. Founded in 1796, Shreve's carries a wide range of fine (if not wildly funky) jewelry, china, home decor, bridal gifts and exclusive Boston souvenirs, like the cunning, must-have swan boat brooch.

Must Be Seen: Nightlife

Grumble, grumble . . . yes, you'll hear some complaining about Boston's early last call (doors close, lights out at 2am). But until then, the city rocks. From funky neighborhood pubs to upscale wine bars, massive dance clubs to tiny live music venues, you'll find plenty of sizzling nightlife to keep you entertained.

Bars & Pubs

Bukowski's Tavern

50 Dalton St., Back Bay. 617-437-9999. Green Line to Prudential Center T stop.

This smallish bar in Back Bay is everything a neighborhood pub should be. Pick from the "99 Bottles of Beer on the Wall" menu (there's actually more than 100 choices) or let the bartender spin the "Wheel of Decision" to make a selection. This is a great after-work, happy-hour hangout, with cheap burgers and fries (try the White Trash Cheese Dip), too. If you come here often, the friendly bartenders really do know your name.

Dad's Beantown Diner

911 Boylston St., Kenmore Square. 617-296-3237. www.2nite.com/dads. Green Line to Kenmore Square T stop.

You'll think you stepped into a *Happy Days* rerun, complete with spinning soda-fountain chairs, neon signs and miles of stainless steel and chrome. This nightspot is a shameless magnet for college students, with two bumping and grinding dance floors, vibrating to top-40 tunes.

Felt

533 Washington St., Downtown. 617-350-5555. www.feltclubboston.com. Green Line to Boston Common T stop.

This combo swank lounge, dance club and upscale pool hall is a downtown hot-spot for the young and well-dressed. DJs spin international house, hip-hop, top-40 and dance music, while people meet on the dance floor, mingle at the bar, or hang around the pool tables. There are live concerts held weekly, too. Very sleek.

Fenway Favorites

Who's On First *(19 Yawkey Way; 617-247-3353; www.whosonfirstboston.com)*, located on the first-base side of Fenway Park, is one of the city's oldest sports bars. Expect crowds on game days; the dance club is popular with local college kids. (If you don't have a ticket to the Red Sox game, use the rear entrance on Brookline Avenue.) Need to commiserate (or celebrate!) with loyal Sox fans? Head to the **Cask 'n Flagon** *(62 Brookline Ave.; 617-536-4840)*, a nitty-gritty bar beyond the legendary Green Monster, or **Boston Beer Works** *(61 Brookline Ave.; 617-536-2337; www.beerworks.net)*, with plenty of big-screen TVs and 16 microbrews.

Jillian's Boston

145 Ipswich St., Kenmore Square. 617-437-0300. www.jilliansboston.com. Green Line to Kenmore Square T stop.

Located behind beloved Fenway Park, this massive, 70,000-square-foot complex features three floors of entertainment. The first floor is home to Tequila Rain restaurant and dance club (think MTV spring break atmosphere); the second floor holds billiard tables, foosball, table tennis and more. On the third floor, you'll find the new upscale Lucky Strike bowling alley, with state-of-the-art lanes, DJ booth, cushy seating and a bar. (This is not your Dad's bowling alley!)

Sing-Along Fun

Sure, it's a little corny. The nightclub act at **Jake Ivory's** *(9 Lansdowne St.; 617-247-1222; www.jakeivorys.com; Kenmore Square T stop)* features dueling piano players banging out 1950s tunes to today's top hits on their baby grand pianos. Sooner or later, you'll be clapping, dancing and singing along. It's a hootin', hollerin' good time.

The Rack

24 Clinton St., at Faneuil Hall, Downtown. 617-725-1051. www.therackboston.com. Green or Orange Line to Faneuil Hall or Haymarket T stop.

A favorite among local athletes and fans, this dressy pool hall and dance club is a mainstay on the Boston night scene. The décor is light and airy, with blond woods, and copper and marble accents. Crowds gather along the long black marble and onyx bar or around the Brunswick Gold Crown pool tables. During the summer, tables are set outside, overlooking Faneuil Hall.

Sonsie

327 Newbury St., Back Bay. 617-351-2500. www.sonsieboston.com. Green Line to Hynes/ ICA T stop.

High-rent Newbury Street, with its profusion of international design boutiques, sports a number of bars and outdoor cafes, but none is more popular than Sonsie. Crowds gather all day long at this stylish cafe to nosh and people watch. When the sun sets, the beautiful people cluster around the long mahogany bar or in the new Red Room lounge, and sip everything from lemon meringues to starfruit martinis.

Irish Pubs

Craving colcannon and Guinness? Well, this is Boston after all; the city is full of the Irish and their favorite pubs. The **Black Rose** *(160 State St.; 617-742-2286; www.irishconnection.com/ blackrose.html)*, located steps from Faneuil Hall, is legendary for its fast-flowing Guinness and live Irish entertainment offered seven days a week. **Charley Flynn's** in the Theater District *(228 Tremont St.; 617-451-5997)* is the quintessential hole-in-the-wall neighborhood pub, perfect for bangers-and-mash-style fare and cold pints.

Dance Clubs

Aria

246 Tremont St., Downtown. 617-338-7080. www.ariaboston.com. Green Line to Boylston T stop.

Sleek, chic and trendy, this black, white and red venue is a showplace for perfectly coiffed and Armani'd international students and the well-heeled young set. Dress up and expect to pay big for champagne and martinis. Thursdays is a favorite midweek event; DJs spin top-40, hip-hop and R&B in different rooms.

Avalon

15 Lansdowne St., Kenmore Square. 617-262-2424. www.avalonboston.com. Green Line to Kenmore Square T stop.

Arguably the best dance club in Boston, this megasize, 2,000-person venue is a longtime favorite. Big, dark, noisy and decadent, Avalon boasts an eclectic schedule of entertainment, from top DJs, live performances and touring rock acts. Expect a young crowd, and be willing to cough up the $15 cover, and to wait in line to do it.

The Big Easy Bar

1 Boylston Pl., Downtown. 617-351-2560. www.bigeasyboston.com. Green Line to Boylston T stop.

Drink up that massive Hurricane and get on the dance floor! This casual, get-down-and-have-some-fun, Bourbon-style club is always lively, drawing a 21-plus crowd of college students and thirtysomethings. There are two lounges (check out the upstairs Crescent Lounge for a quieter atmosphere), four bars and a large wrap-around balcony overlooking the dance floor. DJs spin a mix of blues, rock, pop and funk, depending on the night.

Looking for a Little Romance?

Some of the most romantic spots are tucked away in the dark corners of the city's most elegant hotels. The opulent **Oak Bar at the Fairmont Copley Plaza** *(138 St. James Ave.; 617-267-5300; www.fairmont.com)* is among the best, with its marble bar, gilded ceilings, tall windows, dark wood paneling and plush seats. Sink into one of the corners, then order a chilled carafe of martinis (the bar has one of the largest martini menus in the city). The newly decorated and enlarged **Bristol Lounge at the Four Seasons Hotel** *(200 Boylston St.; 617-338-4400; www.fourseasons.com/boston)* boasts views of the Public Garden, luscious leather couches, a cozy fireplace, and pianists who play classical and jazz nightly.

Caprice

275 Tremont St., Downtown. 617-292-0080. www.capricelounge.com. Green Line to Boylston T stop.

Weekend Latin nights is the claim to fame for this upscale, cosmopolitan lounge. Sip mojitos, and samba or salsa the night away. It's also a popular pre- and post-theater dining spot, since Caprice is located right in the middle of the Theater District.

Roxy

279 Tremont St., Downtown. 617-338-7699. www.roxyplex.com. Green Line to Boylston T stop.

A grand ballroom, balconies and chandeliers harken back to the days when this was once home to the historic Wyndham Tremont Hotel. It remains a favorite with high-energy, dressed-up party-goers who like a lot of bells, whistles and glitter with their music. Saturday nights are legendary and now feature "Cirque du Roxy," with tents, circus props, dueling DJs and a New Year's Eve-style countdown with balloons and confetti drop and a laser show.

Sophia's

1270 Boylston St., Back Bay. 617-351-7001. www.sophiasboston.com. Green Line to Kenmore Square stop.

Sexy low lights and Latin-themed nights make this Fenway-area restaurant and lounge a hotspot with the city's Latino (and wannabes) crowd. You'll find two floors of music and dancing, a cozy champagne lounge and a roof deck that's popular on hot summer nights.

All that Jazz

It might not be huge, but the jazz scene in Boston is high quality. Start at the **Ryles Jazz Club** in Cambridge *(212 Hampshire St. at Inman Square; 617-876-9330; www.rylesjazz.com)*, Boston's premier jazz venue, where big-name musicians like Maynard Ferguson, Jon Hendricks and McCoy Tyler have played. It's as cozy and intimate as a jazz bar should be. The Sunday Jazz Brunch is also popular. Down the street at the Charles Hotel, you'll find the elegant

Regattabar *(1 Bennett St.; 617-876-7777; www.regattabarjazz.com)*, a mainstay on Boston's jazz scene. The 225-seat venue is known for bringing top talent and innovative acts to its stage. Don't let the location (in the DoubleTree Guest Suites) put you off **Scullers** *(400 Soldiers Field Rd.; 617-783-0090; www.scullersjazz.com)*. It remains a top spot for local and national jazz acts. Also popular is Scullers' Supper Club dinner/show package.

re Bostonians too Puritan-practical to enjoy the pleasures of spa-dom? Not a chance! In fact, if you threw a loofah down Newbury Street, you'd probably hit a spa—that's how numerous they are. Given the mean streets (as in pedicure-punishing cobblestones) and harsh climate they have to deal with, Bostonians need—nay, deserve—a fair amount of pampering. At least, that's their excuse! Here's a look at the city's poshest pampering palaces.

Bella Santé

38 Newbury St., Back Bay. 617-424-9930. www.bellasante.com. Arlington T stop.

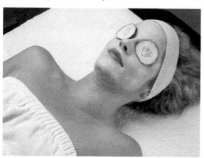

Ultra-homey, with lots of candles and overstuffed couches, Bella Santé is a cocoon of healthy hedonism. Massage, hair removal, body treatments, nail care, facials, and specialized treatments for men are among the services offered. The spa's facials include unusual combos like champagne-and-yeast (for dry, mature skin), and green tea-and-spirulina (for detoxification—if your skin has been staying out and partying too late!). After a day of shopping Newbury Street, who can resist the triple-wax foot massage, followed by peppermint lotion and a pedicure?

Daryl Christopher

37 Newbury St., Back Bay. 617-424-0250. www.dchristopher.com. Arlington T stop.

Be happily mummified in an herbal linen body wrap—the sweetly scented sheets (smelling like Mom left them out on the clothesline to dry) will transport you to a gentler, more relaxing time. The DC organic facial sounds like something you'd eat for breakfast, with ground apricot seeds, oatmeal, and fruit acids extracted from grapefruit and black currant. The feel is New Age-y, the results are wondrous.

Exhale Mind Body Spa

28 Arlington St., Back Bay. 617-532-7000. www.exhalespa.com. Arlington T stop.

One of the newest to hit the Boston scene is this ultra modern New-York-based spa, offering the latest in treatments and exercise programs. The oh-so-serene—nearly spiritual—atmosphere is a welcome sanctuary from the Back Bay hustle and bustle. You'll find a plethora of face and body treatments (all using organic, botanical-based products), an organic cafe, mani-pedi bar, workout rooms and more at this 12,000-square-foot facility, located across from the Public Garden. Exhale's signature CoreFusion mind-body classes, combining core conditioning, Pilates, yoga and stretching, are also offered. On staff are medical experts, dermatologists, even dentists!

G Spa

35 Newbury St., Back Bay. 617-267-4772. www.gspa.biz. Arlington T stop.

Short on time? Step up to the Beauty Bar for a quickie at this very hip Newbury Street spa and boutique. It takes 25 minutes or less for a Quickie Go-2 oxygen facial or Twinkle Toes pedicure. Nails looking a bit ragged? Try the Quickie Manicure; you'll be out in less than 20 minutes and only $15 poorer. There are two floors of products and services, including the more typical, full-scale body, nail, hair and face treatments.

Giuliano Day Spa

338 Newbury St., Back Bay. 617-262-2220. www.giulianodayspa.com/home.php. Hynes/ICA T stop.

After an hour or two here, you'll be sleeker, more gorgeous and a whole lot calmer. They offer the whole spectrum of face and body treatments, plus services like laser hair removal and acupuncture. Another service you won't find everywhere else: The Rasul Signature Room, where you'll be slathered with a mud body mask in an aromatic steam room, then spritzed off in a refreshing rain shower.

Grettacole Spa

At the Westin Copley Place hotel, 10 Huntington Ave., Copley Place, Back Bay. 617-266-6166. www.grettacole.com. Copley T stop.

This "Best of Boston" award winner (according to *Boston Magazine*)—for several years running—is set inside the mall at Copley Place. At the entrance is GrettaLuxe, a small boutique stocked with Prada, Marc Jacobs and Jimmy Choo goodies. Just beyond that are the treatment rooms, where technicians expertly apply custom facials (the deluxe includes glycolic acid, Vitamin C and a seaweed finishing mask) and give make-up lessons using Trish McEvoy products. They offer the full realm of massages, body treatments, hair removal and beauty salon options; the Gretta Body Bronze is a popular choice during Boston's bleak winters.

Le Pli Spa

5 Bennett St., Cambridge. 617-547-4081. www.premierspacollection.com. Harvard Square T stop.

This smallish day spa, located across the river in Cambridge, next to the Charles Hotel *(see Must Stay)*, has been serving Harvard University faculty, Cambridge residents, and visitors for more than 20 years. Recently, it became part of Stonewater Spas. Le Pli lacks the size and amenities (like a steam room, sauna, pool) of some other spas, but offers top-rate services and a full menu. Popular treatments include massages (there's a nice selection to choose from, including hot-stone, deep-tissue and foot), facials and pedicures.

Cambridge★★

Boston's brainy little sister, Cambridge edges the Charles River across from Boston. This oh-so-literate municipality and academic research center is home to renowned **Harvard University★★★**, the **Massachusetts Institute of Technology★** (MIT) and the **Radcliffe Institute for Advanced Study** (formerly Radcliffe College).

> **Touring Tip**
>
> To get your bearings: Massachusetts Avenue ("Mass Ave." to locals) runs the length of Cambridge, extending from Harvard Bridge, past MIT and through Harvard Square. Memorial Drive borders the Charles River.

Chosen as the Bay Colony's capital in 1630, Cambridge has its historic side. Stroll down **Brattle Street★**, where wealthy Tories (loyal to the British Crown) built homes in the 1700s. General George Washington used the house at

no. 105 as his headquarters during the siege of Boston; between 1837 and 1882 poet Henry Wadsworth Longfellow lived in this house, where he penned *Evangeline* (1847) and *The Song of Hiawatha* (1855). Today the home pays homage to the poet as **Longfellow National Historic Site★** *(617-876-4491; www.nps.gov/long; visit by 1-hour guided tour only, Jun–Oct Wed–Sun 10am–4:30pm; $3).*

To the east spreads **Cambridge Common** *(bounded by Garden St. & Massachusetts Ave.)*, the town center for more than 300 years. From 1775 to 1776, it was the site of General Washington's main camp. Off the Common's southwest corner sits **Christ Church** *(Garden St.; 617-876-0200; www.cccambridge.org)*, the oldest church in Cambridge, built in 1760. Today **Harvard Square** *(Massachusetts Ave. & John F. Kennedy St.; www.harvardsquare.com)*, two blocks south of the Common, serves as the city's hub.

Shopping, Cambridge-style

Haute couture isn't part of the dress code on the slushy streets of Cambridge, and with so few parking spaces in town, everybody walks everywhere—so comfortable shoes and a backpack are required.

The Harvard Square area teems with trendy boutiques, eateries, clubs, and book shops like the **Harvard Book Store** *(1256 Mass Ave.; 617-661-1515; www.harvard.com)*. At the **Harvard Coop** *(14 Mass Ave.; 617-499-2000; www.thecoop.com)*, nearly everything has a Harvard or MIT logo on it. Nearby, venerable **Club Passim** *(47 Palmer St.; 617-492-7679; www.clubpassim.org)* showcases big-name folk musicians. Don't miss a stop at **LA Burdick Chocolatiers Café** *(52-D Brattle St.; 617-491-4340; www.burdickchocolate.com)*; the chocolates, pastries and hot chocolate here are to die for!

Too far to walk from Harvard Square, the three-level **CambridgeSide Galleria** *(see map on inside front cover; 100 CambridgeSide Pl.; www.shopcambridgeside.com)* houses some 100 apparel and specialty stores.

Harvard University ★★★

Campus borders the Charles River off Memorial Dr. (west of MIT). 617-495-1000.
www.harvard.edu. Red Line to Harvard T stop.

Harvard is old, really old. The first college established in America, it was founded in 1636 to train young men as leaders of church, state and trade. From 12 students initially, enrollment has grown to some 18,000 degree candidates. In 1879 **Radcliffe College** was founded to provide women with equal access to a Harvard education.

Harvard's superior academic traditions, distinguished faculty and devotion to research have made it one of the world's leading institutions of higher learning. The school's $22.6 billion endowment, the largest of any university in the world, is shared by the undergraduate college and 10 graduate schools. Harvard does not award athletic scholarships or academic credit for physical-education courses, but it does sponsor 40 varsity athletic teams. The university's rowing crews, practicing on the Charles River, are a familiar sight.

A city within a city, Harvard holds some 500 buildings, including more than 100 libraries, 9 museums and dozens of laboratories on 380 acres of land, primarily in Cambridge. Students who live on campus stay in the Harvard Houses, many of them handsome Georgian-style buildings that surround courtyards.

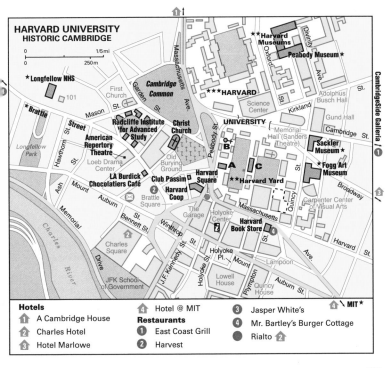

What's What on Harvard's Campus?

Harvard Yard★★ – *Bounded by Mass Ave. & Peabody, Cambridge & Quincy Sts.* The oldest part of the university, Harvard Yard includes **Massachusetts Hall [A]** (1720), the oldest Harvard building still standing; **Holden Chapel [B]**, the university's first official chapel; and **University Hall [C]** (1815), fronted by Daniel Chester French's statue of college founder John Harvard. *Refer to map p 83.*

Touring Tip

Pick up a campus map from the **Events & Information Center**, located in the Holyoke Center Arcade *(1350 Mass. Ave.; 617-495-1573; open year-round Mon–Sat 9am–5pm)*, or take a student-led tour, departing from the center *(Mon–Fri 10am & 2pm, Sat 2pm during the academic year; call for summer hours)*.

Harvard Museum of Natural History★★ – *26 Oxford St. 617-495-3045. www.hmnh.harvard.edu. Open year-round Mon–Sat 9am–5pm. Closed major holidays. $7.50.* Grouped under one roof, four museums hold 21 million specimens and artifacts that make up Harvard's outstanding research collections. Many of the galleries retain the old-fashioned charm of a 19C exhibition hall.

Peabody Museum of Archaeology and Ethnology★ – Founded in 1866, this large museum displays objects and works of art brought back from early 20C expeditions sponsored by Harvard. Highlights include a display exploring the evolution of North American cultures *(ground-floor)*, original plaster casts of pre-Columbian monuments *(3rd floor)*, and the Victorian-style Oceania exhibit *(4th floor)* showcasing well-crafted artifacts from the Pacific Rim. Be sure to stop in the delightful museum shop on the ground floor.

The museums below are accessible from the Peabody's third-floor gallery.

Mineralogical and Geological Museum – Among the numerous minerals, gemstones and meteorites featured in the three galleries here, don't miss the eye-catching giant gypsum crystals from Mexico.

Botanical Museum – The collection of **Blashka Glass Flowers**★★, crafted in Germany by Leopold and Rudolph Blashka between 1886 and 1936, feature nearly 3,000 handblown glass models accurately representing 830 species of flowering plants.

Museum of Comparative Zoology – Some of the rare finds on view in the fossil collections are the 25,000-year-old Harvard mastodon, unearthed in New Jersey; a *Paleosaurus*, one of the oldest fossil dinosaurs (180 million years old); and a *Kronosaurus* (120 million years old), perhaps the largest marine reptile ever to have lived.

Fogg Art Museum★ – *32 Quincy St. 617-495-9400. www.artmuseums.harvard. edu. Open year-round Mon–Sat 10am–5pm, Sun 1pm–5pm. Closed major holidays. $6.50 (includes admission to Busch-Reisinger & Sackler museums).* The Fogg will wow you with Italian Renaissance paintings, Impressionist and post-Impressionist works, and classical art—displayed around a courtyard. The second-floor corridor leads to the adjoining **Busch-Reisinger Museum**★, which spotlights art of 20C German-speaking Europe *(same hours & contact information as Fogg Art Museum).*

Sackler Museum★ – *485 Broadway. Same hours & contact information as Fogg Art Museum. $6.50 (includes admission to Fogg & Busch-Reisinger museums).* This companion museum to the Fogg focuses on Ancient, Near Eastern and Far Eastern Art.

Massachusetts Institute of Technology★

Campus borders the Charles River along Memorial Dr. & Massachusetts Ave. 617-253-1000. www.mit.edu. Red Line to Kendall/MIT T stop.

One of the nation's premier science and research universities, Massachusetts Institute of Technology (MIT) is today a leader in research and development, with schools of Engineering, Science, Architecture and Planning, Management, and Humanities and Social Science. Some 10,000 students from 50 states and 100 foreign countries are enrolled here.

Making the Most of MIT

MIT Museum★ – *265 Massachusetts Ave., Building N52, 2nd Floor. 617-253-4444. http://web.mit.edu/museum. Open year-round Tue–Fri 10am–5pm, weekends noon–5pm. Closed major holidays. $5.* A gadget-lover's delight, this fun house of mind-boggling art includes stop-motion photographs, kinetic sculptures and reputedly the world's largest collection of holograms.

Hart Nautical Collection – *55 Massachusetts Ave., Building 5. 617-253-5942. http://web.mit.edu/museum. Open year-round daily 9am–8pm. Closed major holidays.* Part of the MIT Museum, the Hart gallery displays more than 40 ship models dating from the late 19C through the 20C.

List Visual Arts Center – *20 Ames St., Wiesner Building. 617-253-4680. http://web.mit.edu/lvac. Open Sept–Jun Tue–Sun noon–6pm (Fri until 8pm). Closed major holidays. $5 contribution suggested.* You'll view temporary exhibits of contemporary art here on the main floor of the Wiesner Building, a post-Modern structure designed by MIT graduate I.M. Pei.

Cape Cod and The Islands

Cape Cod★★★

56mi southeast of Boston via I-93 and Rte. 3. Visitor information: Cape Cod Chamber of Commerce Visitor Center, 307 Main St., Hyannis; 508-862-0700; www.capecodchamber.org.

Curling around Cape Cod Bay like a muscular arm in flex, this oddly shaped peninsula juts out into the Atlantic Ocean some 58 miles southeast of Boston. At its fringes, you'll find 300 miles of sandy beaches, fishing villages, salt marshes, dunes covered with sea grass—and in the summer, hordes of people! You might wait several hours to cross the Sagamore Bridge onto the Cape, but once there, you won't be disappointed. During the summer, the bustling towns of **Hyannis** and **Provincetown★★** sizzle with energy. If you prefer more peaceful pleasures, they're here too—tucked down the back roads of **Falmouth★**, atop one of the striking cliffs in Truro, or along spectacular beaches at **Cape Cod National Seashore★★★**.

The Cape is divided into three areas: Upper (Sandwich, Falmouth and Bourne), Mid (Hyannis, Barnstable, Yarmouth, Dennis and Brewster) and Outer (Chatham, Wellfleet, Truro and Provincetown). Highlights in each area begin on p 88.

Touring Tip

If you'd like something handmade as a souvenir, be on the lookout for the hundreds of roadside shops on the Cape, where you can purchase candles, wooden decoys, pottery, glassware and leather goods made by local artisans.

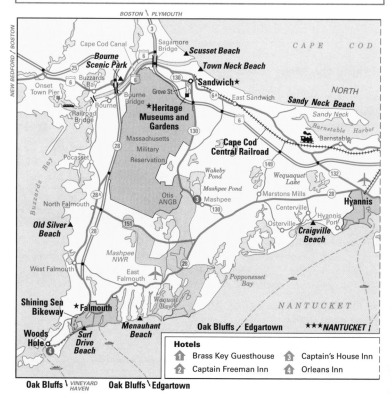

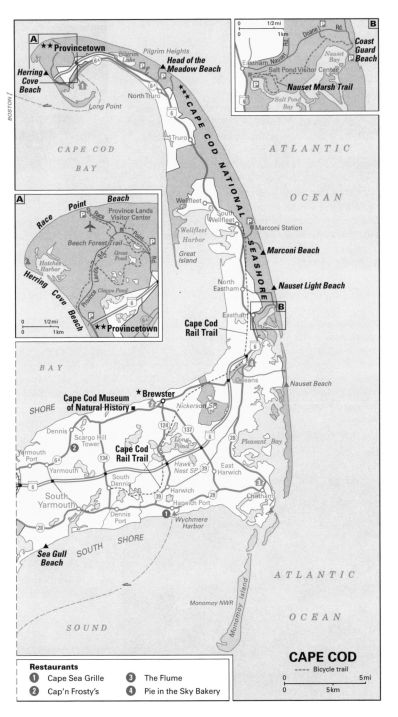

A ★★ **Provincetown**

Herring
Cove
Beach

BOSTON ↑

Pilgrim Heights
Pilgrim Lake
**Head of the
Meadow Beach**

North Truro

Long Point

B

½ mi
1 km

Doane Rd.

Eastham Nauset
Salt Pond Visitor Center

Nauset
Bay

**Coast
Guard
Beach**

Salt Pond
Bay

Nauset Marsh Trail

CAPE COD
BAY

Truro

ATLANTIC

OCEAN

C A P E   C O D   N A T I O N A L

A

Race Point
Beach
Province Lands
Visitor Center
Beech Forest Trail

Race Point

Hatches Harbor

Herring Cove Beach

Great Pond

Province Lands Rd.

Clapps Pond

½ mi
1 km

★★ **Provincetown**

Wellfleet

South
Wellfleet

Wellfleet
Harbor

Great
Island

Marconi Station

Marconi Beach

S E A S H O R E

Nauset Light Beach

North
Eastham

Eastham

B

**Cape Cod
Rail Trail**

Orleans

Nauset Beach

BAY

SHORE

**Cape Cod Museum
of Natural History**

★ **Brewster**

Nickerson SP

Dennis

Scargo Hill
Tower

**Cape Cod
Rail Trail**

Long
Pond

Nickerson SP

Pleasant
Bay

Yarmouth
Port

Yarmouth

South
Dennis

Hawk's
Nest SP

East
Harwich

South
Yarmouth

Dennis
Port

Harwich

Harwich Port

Chatham

**Sea Gull
Beach**

Wychmere
Harbor

S O U T H   S H O R E

ATLANTIC

S O U N D

Monomoy NWR

OCEAN

Monomoy Island

CAPE COD

---- Bicycle trail

5 mi
5 km

Restaurants

1 Cape Sea Grille 3 The Flume

2 Cap'n Frosty's 4 Pie in the Sky Bakery

Upper Cape

Sandwich★

The first settlement on Cape Cod, founded way back in 1637, Sandwich has long been famous for the manufacture of glass. To see glass made here in the 19C, visit the **Sandwich Glass Museum**★ *(129 Main St.; 508-888-0251; www.sandwichglassmuseum.org; open Apr–Dec daily 9:30am–5pm; rest of the year Wed–Sun 9:30am–4pm; closed Jan, Thanksgiving Day & Dec 25; $4.50).* And don't miss a stop at the **Heritage Museums and Gardens**★, featuring an automobile museum, a military museum, an art museum and a large rhododendron garden *(Rte. 6A at Grove & Pine Sts.; 508-888-3300; www.heritagemuseumsandgardens.org; open May–Oct daily 9am–6pm; rest of the year call for hours; $12).*

Woods Hole

At the southwest tip of the Upper Cape, two miles beyond lovely **Falmouth**★, lies the former whaling port of Woods Hole. The **Shining Sea Bikeway** links the two towns *(for details, contact the town of Falmouth; 508-548-7611; www.townfalmouth.ma.us).* Today Woods Hole is a world center for the study of marine life. Two private laboratories, two federal marine facilities and a science aquarium are located here, as well as the largest independent marine-research lab in the US, **Woods Hole Oceanographic Institution** *(508-289-2252; www.whoi.edu; 1-hour tours Jul & Aug Mon–Fri 10:30am & 1:30pm; reservations required).* The small town is also the departure point for ferries to **Martha's Vineyard**★★ *(see p 92).*

Upper Cape Beaches

Need a place to set up your beach chair? **Scusset Beach**, though not actually on the Cape itself, occupies a pleasant stretch of sand on the Cape Cod Canal; also on the Canal, **Bourne Scenic Park** boasts 70 acres for hiking, fishing and

lake swimming. **Town Neck Beach**, on the bayside in Sandwich, offers pretty views and good swimming. Other fine beaches include **Surf Drive Beach** on Vineyard Sound in Falmouth, **Old Silver Beach** on Buzzard's Bay in North Falmouth, and **Menauhant Beach** on Vineyard Sound in East Falmouth.

Mid-Cape

Brewster★

A charmer on the North Shore, the resort town of Brewster was first settled in the mid-17C. Many of the stately residences you'll see were built by prosperous sea captains in the 19C. Be sure to visit the **Cape Cod Museum of Natural History** *(869 Main St.; 508-896-3867; www.ccmnh.org; open Apr–May Wed–Sun 10am–4pm; Jun–Sept daily 10am–4pm; rest of the year weekends 10am–4pm; closed major holidays; $7)*, where you'll find interactive exhibits on the plants, animals and geology of the Cape. Take one of the three nature trails on the property *(grounds open year-round daily)* to explore salt marshes, cranberry bogs and a pristine beach.

Touring Tip

Part of the fun on Cape Cod is a stop at a general store, a common roadside sight throughout New England. Enter the **Brewster General Store** *(1935 Main St.; 508-896-3744; www.brewsterstore.com)* and you step into a world of Americana, past and present. Get your beach and picnic supplies here, and about anything else you need. Oh, and an ice-cream cone too, of course.

Hyannis

Looking for action? You'll find it in this South Shore town. It's the major shopping center for the Cape and the hub of airline and ferry services. There are plenty of souvenir shops and places to eat (don't overlook the seafood shacks). At the Hyannis Depot, you can board a 1920s parlor car for a two-hour scenic tour offered by the **Cape Cod Central Railroad** *(252 Main St.; 508-771-3800; www.capetrain.com)*, with stops at Sandwich and the Cape Cod Canal.

Mid-Cape Beaches

Sandy Neck Beach *(Sandy Neck Rd., in Barnstable)* is considered one of the best public beaches on the Cape. The shallow pools formed here at low tide delight children. Surrounded by dunes and salt marshes, Sandy Neck has great views, to boot. On Nantucket Sound, **Sea Gull Beach** *(off South St., in Yarmouth)* is another winner; calm waters here make for great swimming. It's the largest beach in Yarmouth.

Touring Tip

If you have teens or preteens in your group, they'll enjoy the scene at popular **Craigville Beach**, with its gentle surf and warm water. MTV crews have shown up in the past to film here. Need we say more?

Outer Cape

Cape Cod National Seashore★★★

Along the Cape's outer arm, some 400 miles of coastline are federally protected as a national seashore. Choose from several beaches here (lifeguards are on duty in summer): **Coast Guard Beach**, **Nauset Light Beach**, **Marconi Beach**, **Head of the Meadow Beach**, **Race Point Beach** and **Herring Cove Beach**. A visitor center *(call the National Park Service for hours)* is located at each end of the 27,000-acre seashore. *For parking passes and details, call 508-349-3785 or visit www.nps.gov/caco.*

Cycling the Cape

Cape Cod Rail Trail follows a paved former rail bed for 19.6 miles from South Dennis to the Salt Pond Visitor Center in Eastham, or 25.8 miles to South Wellfleet *(for information and maps, contact Nickerson State Park: 508-896-3491 or www.mass.gov).* **Nauset Marsh Trail** winds 1.6 miles from the Salt Pond Visitor Center through marshland to Coast Guard Beach. The staff at the Cape Cod National Seashore *(above)* can provide details.

Provincetown★★

The site of the Pilgrims' first landing, in November 1620, bustling P-Town is today one happening place. It's chock-full of art galleries, shops, dance clubs, bars, restaurants, a theater company—and hordes of summer visitors, especially gays and lesbians. Surrounded on three sides by beaches on the northern tip of Cape Cod *(see Cape Cod National Seashore, above),* the town abounds with opportunities for kayaking, biking, hiking, sailing and windsurfing.

Pilgrim Monument & Provincetown Museum★ – *High Pole Hill Rd. 508-487-1310. www.pilgrim-monument.org. Open Apr–Nov daily 9am–4:15pm (Jul–Aug until 6:15pm). Closed Thanksgiving Day. $7.* You can't miss this granite structure, built to commemorate the Pilgrims' 1620 landing here—it towers 252 feet above the town. Climb the 166 steps, and you'll be rewarded with sweeping views of P-town, its harbor and the lower Cape. You enter the tower through the small museum, where you'll see a model of the *Mayflower.*

Where the Wild Things Are

One of the best things to do on the Cape? Jump on a whale-watching cruise to Stellwagen Bank, a popular feeding ground for whales; several P-town outfitters offer trips throughout the summer. Come winter, dress warmly and board a boat for a seal-watching trip offered by the Massachusetts Audubon Society's Wellfleet Bay Wildlife Sanctuary *(291 State Hwy., Rte. 6, South Wellfleet; 508-349-2615; www.massaudubon.org).*

Nantucket★★★

28mi south of Hyannis. Access by ferry (see sidebar below) or plane. Visitor information: Nantucket Island Chamber of Commerce, 48 Main St., Nantucket; 508-228-1700; www.nantucketchamber.org.

In the Algonquian language, Nantucket means "far-away land," but this island, once the premier summer resort destinations on the East Coast, lies a mere 28 miles off the Cape. Step off the ferry into almost perfectly preserved **Nantucket village★★★**, a 19C enclave of cobblestone streets and redbrick mansions. From 1740 to the 1830s, Nantucket reigned as the world's foremost whaling port. Merchants and ship owners who grew rich selling precious whale oil built the magnificent homes lining **Main Street★★★** near the wharves. Elegant sea captains' homes now house fine restaurants, boutiques and inns.

To Nantucket by Boat

The ferries of the **Steamship Authority** *(508-477-8600; www.steamshipauthority.com)* carry cars, passengers, pets and bikes year-round from Hyannis to Nantucket, a 2-hour-and-15-minute trip, or one hour by high-speed ferry *(no cars or pets; reservations: 508-495-3278)*. **Hy-Line Cruises** offers seasonal two-hour service and year-round one-hour high-speed catamaran service from Hyannis; no cars allowed *(508-778-2600; www.hy-linecruises.com; call 800-492-8082 for high-speed-service reservations)*. **Freedom Cruise Line** *(508-432-8999; www.nantucketislandferry.com)* carries passengers and bikes, and departs from Harwich Port daily late May–mid-October.

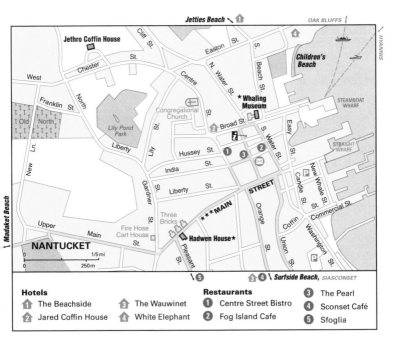

Hotels

- 🛏 1 The Beachside
- 🛏 2 Jared Coffin House
- 🛏 3 The Wauwinet
- 🛏 4 White Elephant

Restaurants

- 1 Centre Street Bistro
- 2 Fog Island Cafe
- 3 The Pearl
- 4 Sconset Café
- 5 Sfoglia

Cape Cod and The Islands

Historic Sites

Your ticket from the **Nantucket Historical Association** *(7 Fair St.; 508-228-1894; www.nha.org)* includes a 90-minute guided walking tour of the town, and admission to several historic properties *(open Memorial Day–Labor Day Mon–Sat 10am–5pm; call for off-season hours; $15; purchase tickets at any of the following sites)*. Sites include the **Hadwen House**★ *(96 Main St.)*, built in 1845 for a whale-oil merchant; and the **Jethro Coffin House** *(Sunset Hill)*, one of the few remaining structures from the 17C English settlement.

The **Whaling Museum**★ *(15 Broad St.)* contains wonderful collections of scrimshaw, harpoons, ships models and an impressive skeleton of a 46-foot sperm whale. It reopens to the public in spring 2005 after a significant renovation. Step inside the re-created blacksmith shop, sail loft, and cooper's shop to see trades and crafts relating to the whaling industry.

Nantucket Beaches

Jetties Beach and **Children's Beach**, both on the north shore, are ideal for kids. Jetties has changing rooms, showers, a snack bar and boat rentals; Children's features a playground and picnic area. On the south shore, **Surfside Beach** is popular with beachcombers, kite-flyers and surfcasters. **Madaket Beach**, at the island's west end, gets pounded by heavy surf, but the sunsets there are spectacular.

Martha's Vineyard★★

7mi south of Hyannis. Access via ferry (see sidebar below) or plane. Visitor information: Martha's Vineyard Chamber of Commerce on Beach Rd., Vineyard Haven; 508-693-0085 or 800-505-4815; www.mvy.com.

Actually, you'll find few vineyards on this triangular-shaped island, off the south coast of Cape Cod. You will find broad beaches, small fishing villages and summer resorts, shops, restaurants and attractions. The population of Martha's Vineyard skyrockets in the summer, bringing a mix of day-trippers, vacationers and wealthy second-home owners.

To Martha's Vineyard by Boat

The **Steamship Authority** *(508-477-8600; www.steamshipauthority.com)* offers ferry service from Woods Hole daily year-round to Oak Bluffs and Vineyard Haven. This is the only line that accommodates cars and trucks. The **Island Queen** *(508-548-4800; www.islandqueen.com)* offers seasonal daily walk-on, passenger-only service from Falmouth to Oak Bluffs. **Hy-line Cruises** *(508-778-2600; www.hy-linecruises.com)* offers seasonal daily walk-on, passenger-only service from Hyannis to Oak Bluffs.

Gay Head Cliffs★★

Famous for their blue, tan, gray, red and orange hues, these 100-million-year-old, 60-foot-high clay cliffs contain fossils of prehistoric camels, wild horses and ancient whales. Today Gay Head's Native American residents use the clay to make decorative pottery.

Edgartown★

Pleasure craft crowd Edgartown Harbor, once filled with whaling vessels in the 19C. To get an idea of the town's past, visit the **Vineyard Museum** *(Cooke & School Sts.; 508-627-4441; www.marthasvineyardhistory.org)*, where historic houses showcase maritime and Native American artifacts.

Oak Bluffs★

In the 1830s the Methodists met in an oak grove here. Eventually some 12,000 people were attending annual services at **Cottage City**, as the encampment came to be known (later renamed Oak Bluffs). Today you can see the Victorian gingerbread houses built to replace tents that stood near the tabernacle. Then take a spin on the **Flying Horses Carousel** *(Oak Bluffs Ave.; 508-693-9481; www.mvpreservation.org/carousel.html; open Easter Sat–Columbus Day; $1)*.

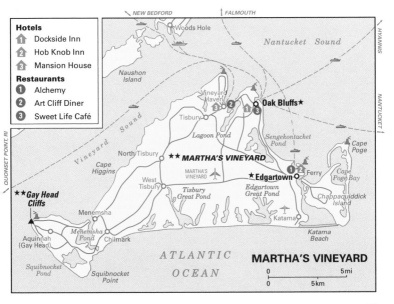

Best Excursions from Boston

Yet another great thing about Boston: a host of worthy day trips lie only an hour's drive or so away. Head north to Salem and Cape Ann, west to Lexington, Concord and Sturbridge, and south to New Bedford and Plymouth (home of that famous rock). You might encounter witches, Colonial villagers or Minutemen among the locals! Heading east will just get you . . . wet!

Old Sturbridge Village★★★

58mi southwest of Boston in Sturbridge. Take I-90 (Mass. Tpk.) west to Exit 9. Turn right after the tolls onto Rte. 20 West; after a half-mile, turn right. 508-347-3362 or 800-733-1830. www.osv.org. Open Apr–Oct daily 9am–5pm (Jul & weekends until 6pm). Rest of the year, call for hours. Closed Dec 25. $20 (2nd consecutive day free).

If you want to escape the modern world for a day, come to this living-history museum that re-creates life between 1790 and 1840 in rural New England. You'll find yourself ambling in and out of historic houses, farm buildings and shops moved here or constructed on the site. You can watch interpreters in 19C dress farm the land and make tools the old-fashioned way. Seasonal activities—like picking apples in the fall or shearing sheep in spring—are yours for the choosing. *Pick up a site map and a schedule of events at the entrance.*

The village was initiated by Albert and Joel Cheney Wells and their families to exhibit their collections of American antiques. When the museum was opened to the public in 1946, historic houses, farm buildings and shops had been moved to and reconstructed on the Sturbridge site.

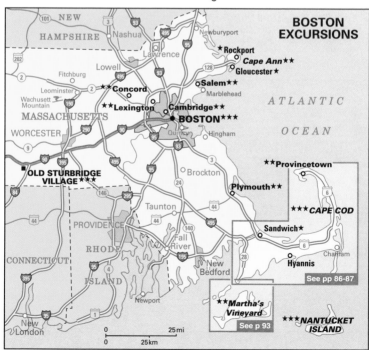

A Slice of Village Life

Freeman Farm – You'll see "farmers" plowing, milking cows, building fences and performing other farm activities.

Knight Store – This well-stocked mercantile is typical of the country store that was often the sole supplier of the farmer's needs.

Printing Office – Offices such as this one usually printed books, pamphlets and broadsides (a printed page for posting or distributing).

Tin Shop – Watch a "smithy" turn out practical wares like those used in early-19C households.

Touring Tip: Take the Kids

If you have children in tow, visit the **Samson's Children's Museum**, a space designed for children under 8 years of age, where they can try on costumes, test their cooking skills or design a quilt. Kids of all ages are welcome at **Kidstory**, a discovery gallery featuring activities that re-create chores performed in the village.

Cape Ann★★

37mi north of Boston. Take US-1 north to I-95/Rte. 128. Take Exit 45, and continue east on Rte. 128 to Gloucester. Visitor information: 978-977-7760 or www.northofboston.org.

The "other Cape" has much to recommend it—salty sea air, fishing villages, coastal estates and rocky harbors. Take the 32-mile road *(Rtes. 127 & 127A)* that rings the periphery of Cape Ann for stunning views of the beaches and towns—including **Gloucester★**, the oldest seaport in the nation. Below are a couple of good places to get out and wander.

Cape Ann Historical Museum★★

27 Pleasant St., Gloucester. 978-283-0455. www.capeannhistoricalmuseum.org. Open Mar–Jan Tue–Sat 10am–5pm. Closed major holidays. $4.

Three levels of sunlit galleries trace the history of the maritime industries here, and highlight works of 19C and 20C artists such as Winslow Homer and Fitz Hugh Lane, who were drawn to Cape Ann's light and landscape.

Rockport★

Follow 127A (Thatcher Rd.) to South St. In-town parking is difficult in summer season, but a shuttle bus operates every 15min between the parking lot outside town and the town center.

This former fishing village evolved as an artists' colony in the 1920s. The red fishing shack **Motif Number 1★** is the most photographed scene in America, so they say. Wander around **Bearskin Neck★**, where old fishing sheds have been converted into shops and galleries.

Concord and Lexington★★

Lexington and Concord have been linked in the minds of Americans since April 19, 1775, the day British and colonial troops clashed here, triggering the American Revolution. At the Revolutionary War sites preserved in these two neighboring cities, you can retrace the incidents that occurred on that day. In the 19C, Concord was home to writers Ralph Waldo Emerson and Henry David Thoreau.

Concord★★

17mi west of Boston. Leave Boston over the Longfellow Bridge. Take Memorial Drive west through Cambridge, where it becomes US-3/Rte. 2. Continue west on Rte. 2 (Concord Tpk.) to Rte. 126/Walden St. in Concord. Visitor information: 978-369-3120 or www.concordmachamber.org.

Concord Museum★ – *Lexington Rd. & Cambridge Turnpike. 978-369-9609. www.concordmuseum.org. Open Apr–Dec Mon–Sat 9am–5pm, Sun noon–5pm. Rest of the year Mon–Sat 11am–4pm, Sun 1pm–4pm. Closed major holidays. $8.* The artifacts, documents and period rooms here give you a sense of Concord's rich history. You'll see a lantern hung in the steeple of Old North Church *(see Landmarks)* to signal Paul Revere, and objects used by Thoreau at Walden Pond *(opposite)*.

Minute Man National Historical Park★ – *Visitor Center located off Rte. 2A in Lexington. 978-369-6993. www.nps.gov/mima.* This park commemorates the events that took place on April 19, 1775, along Battle Road (Rte. 2A between Lexing- ton and Concord) and in Lexington, Lincoln and Concord. Take the interpretive trail that runs alongside Battle Road to learn about the Patriots' guerrilla-style attacks on British troops retreating to Bunker Hill.

- **North Bridge Unit★★** – A replica of the **Old North Bridge★** marks the place where colonial farmers advanced on the British and fired the "shot heard 'round the world." Emerson immortalized the bridge in his poem *Concord Hymn*. Nearby, Daniel Chester French's statue of the **Minute Man [1]** *(refers to map p 97)* honors the Patriots who resisted the British at Concord.

Sleepy Hollow Cemetery –
*Bedford St. at Partridge Lane.
From Concord center, turn right
onto Rte. 62. Enter the cemetery
through the second gate on the
left and follow signs for Author's
Ridge. 978-318-3233. Open year-
round daily 7am–dusk.* A short
climb from the parking lot leads
to Author's Ridge, where the
Alcotts, Nathaniel Hawthorne,
Ralph Waldo Emerson, Henry
David Thoreau, Margaret Sydney
and others are buried.

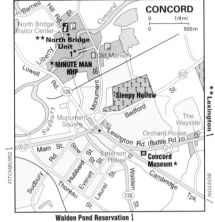

Walden Pond Reservation –
*1.5mi south of Concord center on
Rte. 126 (Walden St.).* Henry David Thoreau built his cabin on the shore of
this lake. To reach the cabin site (marked by a pile of stones) from the
parking lot, follow the trail signs to a granite post, where the trail turns right
(a 15-minute walk).

Lexington★★

*7.5mi east of Concord on Rte. 2A. Visitor information: 781-862-2480 or
www.lexingtonchamber.org. Visitor center located at 1875 Massachusetts Ave.*

Lexington Green★★ – The first confrontation between the British soldiers
and the Minutemen on April 19 took place in this triangular park. Henry
Kitson's statue **The Minuteman** represents the
leader of the Lexington militia, Captain Parker.
Seven of the colonists killed here that day are
buried beneath the Revolutionary Monument.

Buckman Tavern★ – *1 Bedford St. 781-862-
5598. www.lexingtonhistory.org. Visit by 30min
guided tour only, Apr–mid-Nov Mon–Sat
10am–5pm, Sun noon–5pm (summer until 6pm).
$5.* The Minutemen gathered here on April 18
to await the arrival of British troops. Patriots
wounded in the ensuing battle with the British
on the green were carried to Buckman Tavern
for medical care.

Minute Man Visitor Center★ – *Off Rte. 2A in Lexington. 978-369-6993.
www.nps.gov/mima. Open mid-Apr–Oct daily 9am–5pm. Rest of the year daily
9am–4pm. Closed Jan 1 & Dec 25.* Exhibits and a state-of-the-art multimedia
presentation entitled *The Road to Revolution (25min)* trace the events of
April 19, 1775.

Plymouth★★

41mi southeast of Boston. Take I-93 south from Boston to Exit 7/20. Continue south on Rte. 3 to Exit 9, and take Rte. 3A into Plymouth. Visitor Center at 130 Water St. 508-747-7533 or 800-872-1620. www.visit-plymouth.com. Open Jul–Aug daily 8am–8pm. Sept–Nov & Apr–Jun daily 9am–5pm.

This attractive town, with hilly streets sloping down to the harbor, is the site of the first permanent settlement in New England. The long voyage of the *Mayflower*, the hardships that the Pilgrims endured and the eventual success of Plymouth Colony form part of the cherished story related in Plymouth's historic monuments and sites.

Plimoth Plantation★★

3mi south on Rte. 3 from the center of Plymouth; take Exit 4. 508-746-1622. www.plimoth.org. Open Apr–late-Nov daily 9:30am–5pm. $20 ($22 including Mayflower II).

This reproduction of the Pilgrims' village as it appeared in 1627 really looks authentic. Why is the plantation spelled "Plimoth?" The museum curators adopted this spelling from colonial Governor William Bradford's early journals.

Highlights here include **The Dwellings**, rows of thatched-roof cottages similar to those inhabited by the Alden, Carver, Bradford, Standish and other families; the **Hobbamock's Wampanoag Indian Homesite**, where staff members interpret the culture of the Wampanoag people; and the **Carriage House Crafts Center**, where you can watch as workers use 17C methods to make handicrafts. The **Fort/Meetinghouse**, at the entrance to the plantation, is the best vantage point for a view of the entire village.

Mayflower II★★

Berthed at the State Pier. 508-746-1622. www.plimoth.org. Open Apr–Nov daily 9am–5pm. $8 ($22 combination ticket includes Plimoth Plantation).

The *Mayflower II*, built in England in 1957, is a full-scale replica of the ship that carried the Pilgrims to Plymouth in 1620. Now it seems so small!

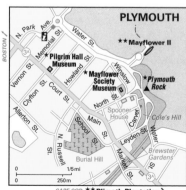

Mayflower Society Museum★

4 Winslow St. 508-746-2590.
www.mayflower.org/museum. Visit by 40min
guided tour only, Jul–Aug daily 10am–4pm.
Rest of the year Fri–Sun 10am–4pm. Closed
major holidays. $4.

Among the antiques inside this
museum, built during the colonial
period and enlarged in the 19C, look for
a rare set of biblical fireplace tiles in
the drawing room.

Pilgrim Hall Museum★

75 Court St. 508-746-1620. www.pilgrimhall.org. Open Feb–Dec daily 9:30am–4:30pm.
Closed Dec 25. $6.

Built as a memorial to the Pilgrims, this austere 1824 structure contains original
Pilgrim furnishings and artifacts, including the cradle of Peregine White, who
was born on the *Mayflower*.

Plymouth Rock★

On the beach at Water St.

It's not what you expect to see—the famous boulder enclosed in a columned
structure at the water's edge. Since it's regarded as the stepping stone used by
the *Mayflower* passengers when they disembarked at Plymouth, the treasured
rock must be protected for posterity!

Salem★★

15mi northeast of Boston. Take Rte. 1A
north from Boston to Rte. 60 in Revere.
Continue north to Rte. 107 and follow it
north to Salem. Visitor information:
877-725-3662 or www.salem.org.

Say the name Salem, and witchcraft
springs to mind. The seaside city
capitalizes on its history as a 17C town
tormented by the fear of witches.
Several points of interest re-create
the witch-hunts, and some shops sell
witchcraft items. At Halloween the
city hosts a 10-day festival called
Haunted Happenings. Visitors come
to Salem for its maritime heritage as
well. After all, it was once a bustling
seaport that launched 1,000 ships.

Witchcraft Hysteria

In 1692 several young girls, their imagi-
nations stirred by tales of voodoo told
to them by the West Indian slave
Tituba, began to have visions and con-
vulsive fits. After examining the girls, a
doctor declared them to be victims of
"the evil hand." The frightened girls
accused Tituba and two other women
of having bewitched them; the women
were arrested and jailed. In the frenzy
of fear that followed, more than 200
persons were accused of witchcraft;
150 were imprisoned and 19 found
guilty and hanged. The hysteria, credit-
ed in retrospect to rivalries between
several prominent Salem families, came
to an abrupt end a year later when
Governor William Phips' wife was
accused of witchcraft.

Peabody Essex Museum★★★

East India Square. 800-745-9500. www.pem.org. Open year-round daily 10am–5pm (Thu until 9pm). Closed Jan 1, Thanksgiving Day & Dec 25. $13. Additional charge for Yin Yu Tang: A Chinese House.

This illustrious museum just keeps getting better. From its beginnings in 1799 as the Salem East India Marine Society's meeting hall to the present facility with its striking new wing (2003), the Peabody Essex Museum has become one of the largest museums on the East Coast. Collections focus on America's maritime history from the 17C to the present, and on Salem's past, including the city's heady days in the 18C and 19C, when ship captains returned with porcelain, carvings and other treasures from the Far East, India, Africa and the Pacific Islands. The museum has one of

the most complete collections of Asian export art in the world, and counts historic houses and an extensive research library as part of its complex.

Historic Houses

Several historic houses worth a tour, including the following, are located near the museum *(entry fee included in museum admission)*: **Gardner-Pingree House**★★ **[A]**, a handsome brick mansion built in 1805; **John Ward House** ★ **[B]** (1684), an example of 17C American Colonial architecture; and **Crowninshield-Bentley House [C]**, a 1730 dwelling typical of mid-18C New England architecture. The remarkable **Yin Yu Tang** *($4)*, a traditional early-19C Chinese merchant's house, was relocated here, with its original furnishings, from southeast China. *[A], [B] and [C] refer to the map on p 101.*

Peeling Back the Peabody

American Decorative Arts – Furnishings, paintings, textiles, toys and costumes from the colonial period through the early 20C make up this impressive collection.

Asian Export Art – Fine examples of 19C and early-20C porcelain, silver, furniture and textiles created in China, Japan, India, the Philippines and Ceylon (now Sri Lanka) are exhibited.

Asian, African and Pacific Islands Art – Textiles, shields, ritual costumes, masks and pottery from the tropical Pacific Islands, Indonesia, Japan and Africa fill this gallery, along with 19C Meiji costumes from Japan.

Maritime Art and History – Here you'll find paintings by Fitz Hugh Lane, John Singleton Copley and Gilbert Stuart; ships' portraits commissioned by the vessels' owners; and rare nautical instruments and carved ships' figureheads.

Native American Arts and Archaeology – Artifacts here come from the Indian cultures of the Eastern seaboard, Great Lakes, Great Plains, Northwest Coast and South America.

Natural History – The collection represents flora and fauna, mainly from the eastern US.

House of the Seven Gables★

54 Turner St. 978-744-0991. www.7gables.org. Visit by 45min guided tour only, Jul–Oct daily 10am–7pm. Rest of the year daily 10am–5pm. Closed Jan 1, Thanksgiving Day & Dec 25. Closes at 2pm Dec. 24 & Dec 31. $11.

A leading 19C American literary figure, **Nathaniel Hawthorne** (1804-1864) was born in Salem, which provided the setting for many of his works. Hawthorne's novel of the same name immortalized this rambling three-story Colonial house, built in 1668. Tours include the author's birthplace (c.1750).

Salem Maritime National Historic Site★

174 Derby St. 978-740-1660. www.nps.gov/sama. Open year-round daily 9am–5pm. Closed Jan 1, Thanksgiving Day & Dec 25.

Visit the city's historic waterfront to relive Salem's glory days. Of the 40 wharves that once reached out into the harbor, **Derby Wharf**, the longest (2,100 feet), remains. Guided tours *($5)* of the site include the **Custom House★**, where Nathaniel Hawthorne worked as a port officer; the **Derby House** (1762); and a replica of the merchant vessel **Friendship**.

New Bedford Whaling Museum★★

60mi south of Boston in New Bedford. Take I-93 south from Boston to Exit 4/21. Drive south on Rte. 24 to Exit 12; continue south on Rte. 140 to New Bedford. To reach the museum, take I-195 east to Rte. 18; drive south to the downtown exit. 18 Johnny Cake Hill. 508-997-0046. www.whalingmuseum.org. Open year-round daily 9am–5pm. Closed Jan 1, Thanksgiving Day & Dec 25. $10.

Interested in whaling? The museum's collections of artifacts, prints, log books and journals are among the world's finest. Paintings, scrimshaw, sailor's Valentines and more illustrate the history of whaling.

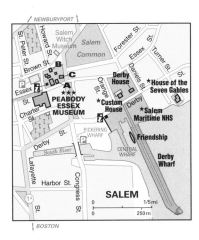

The venues below were selected for their ambience, location and/or value for money. Rates indicate the average cost of an appetizer, an entrée and a dessert for one person (not including tax, gratuity or beverages). Most restaurants are open daily (except where noted) and accept major credit cards. Call for information regarding reservations, dress code and opening hours. For a selected listing of restaurants by theme (Outdoor Dining, Star Chefs, etc.), see p 113. Properties in this section are located in Boston unless otherwise noted.

$$$$	Over $50	**$$**	$15–$30
$$$	$30–$50	**$**	Under $15

Luxury

Aujourd'hui $$$$ French

200 Boylston St., in the Four Seasons Hotel, Back Bay. Dinner & Sun brunch only. 617-338-4400. www.fourseasons.com.

The formal, boardroom-like atmosphere of the Four Season's signature restaurant stands in sharp contrast to chef Jerome Legras' playful, adventurous food. Not everywhere do you find crab foam or Parmesan cheesecake on your appetizer plate. Call it a fusion of French and Japanese, in which precise squares of fish are drizzled with amazing butter-based sauces. Try the horseradish-crusted halibut with fava-bean ragout, porcini and roasted-fish jus, and see why Aujourd'hui remains one of the city's standout dining rooms.

Great Bay $$$$ Seafood

500 Commonwealth Ave., in the Hotel Commonwealth, Kenmore Square. No lunch weekends. 617-532-5300. www.hotelcommonwealth.com.

A pancake house once stood on this spot across from Boston University; now, there's a sleek, narrow dining room where restaurateurs Michael Schlow and Chris Myers pay homage to fish. Exotic and local seafood meet on the menu here—some cooked, some raw—including offerings like Japanese octopus and coriander-crusted Spanish mackerel with a pomegranate purée. Don't pass up the spicy halibut tacos, served with papaya salsa.

Grill 23 & Bar $$$$ American

161 Berkeley St., Back Bay. 617-542-2255. www.grill23.com.

Filled with martini-quaffing power suits, this clubby Back Bay haven has welcomed expense-account customers for some 20 years. The restaurant built its reputation on its top-quality steaks, but Grill 23 has also made its mark as a seafood destination. Preparations range from straightforward filet mignon, New York sirloin or grilled swordfish to more imaginative choices that might include cedar-roasted salmon with a warm snap-pea and potato salad. The award-winning 900-label wine list includes reds from French Bordeaux to super Tuscans from Italy.

Hamersley's Bistro $$$$ French

553 Tremont St., South End. Dinner only. 617-423-2700. www.hamersleysbistro.com.

Hamersley's helped establish the South End as a prime dining destination, and this petite bistro, where patrons turn up in everything from sweaters to suits, is still going strong. The seasonal menu stresses creative comfort food with a French flair, from its wholesome cassoulet to the signature garlicky roast chicken. Hamersley's caters to non-meat eaters with a three-course vegetarian tasting menu ($35). The dining area is small, but cheery, with buttercolored walls. Stop by in summer for a bite outside on the patio.

Mantra $$$$ French

52 Temple Pl., Downtown. Closed Sun. 617-542-8111. www.mantrarestaurant.com.

Set in a renovated bank building, this eatery is perhaps best known for its hookah den, where it's all about tapas, cocktails and canoodling, not opium!). Co-chefs Ernie Quinones and Philip Carolan have created a happy mix of Indian-influenced French dishes, including spice-crusted tuna with eggplant caviar, arugula and a pinot noir reduction. The bar menu is first-rate, too.

Radius $$$$ French

8 High St., Downtown. Closed Sun. 617-426-1234. www.radiusrestaurant.com.

One of Boston's top tables, this sleek Financial District dining room exudes a mix of efficiency and Zen-like composure, from the staff's Nehru-style jackets to the artfully prepared contemporary French fare. Business types share space with foodies here, but the opulent experience comes at a price. The menu brims with luxury ingredients: seared foie gras with tropical fruits, Maine diver scallops with heirloom squash and black trumpet mushrooms, or Colorado lamb paired with barley risotto. Tempting finales include warm palm-ginger cakes with chilled pineapple soup, and Tahitian-vanilla crème brûlée.

Rialto $$$$ Mediterranean

In the Charles Hotel, One Bennett St., Cambridge. Dinner only. 617-661-5050. www.rialto-restaurant.com.

Consistently ranked among the Boston area's top restaurants, Rialto serves up epicurean elegance in a snazzy setting, with striped lampshades and two-toned wood floors complementing curvaceous Art Deco-style seating and floor-to-ceiling windows. Chef Jody Adams' food derives its inspiration from southern Europe, updated with Boston panache: Expect savory seafood dishes, pastas and game prepared with seasonal vegetables and plated with artful precision. Save room for the rich chèvre cheesecake or the decadent Three Degrees of Chocolate.

Moderate

Durgin-Park $$$ New England

340 Faneuil Hall Marketplace, Downtown. 617-227-2038. www.durgin-park.com.

"There's no place like this place anywhere near this place, so this must be the place," reads the notice at the entrance, and it's true. For more than 130 years, Durgin-Park has exuded a quirky charm, while serving slices of roast beef that are approximately the size of your head, Boston baked beans, cornbread and other hearty fare. Although the wait staff doesn't insult customers like they used to (they will if you give them a hard time—which we don't recommend), they're hardly mellow. Nevertheless, diners sitting at communal tables pass dishes around and enjoy the unpretentious food and bustling atmosphere.

Harvest $$$ New England

44 Brattle St., Cambridge. Dinner & Sun brunch only. 617-868-2255. www.theharvest.com.

Salt-and-pepper-colored upholstery punctuates the corn-yellow walls and dark woods in this classy space in Harvard Square. The landmark restaurant draws students, visiting parents, and tweedy professorial types who appreciate its subdued elegance and good value. New England bounty is served with contemporary flair: Nantucket Bay scallop bisque; roasted cod served with navy beans, rock shrimp and grilled squid; and rack of pork with rainbow chard and Cape Cod cranberries.

Jasper White's Summer Shack $$$ Seafood

50 Dalton St., Back Bay; 617-867-9955. Also at 149 Alewife Brook Pkwy., Cambridge; 617-520-9500. www.summershackrestaurant.com.

Only a few chefs get over-the-title billing; Jasper White is one of them. He took over the barnlike space of Aku Aku in Cambridge and turned it into a kitschy roadside diner, serving the likes of clambakes and corn dogs to rave reviews. The long lines attest to the popularity of the place, which gets the B52s-type ambience (lime-green booths, funky signage) and the menu just right. There's nothing "shacky" about the prices, but you do get that Jasperian touch, which elevates simple summertime fare to sublime levels.

Kingfish Hall $$$ Seafood

188 Faneuil Hall Marketplace, Downtown. 617-523-8862. www.toddenglish.com.

Chef Todd English (of Olives fame) segued into seafood with this flashy fish emporium at Faneuil Hall. Its location lures a mixed crowd, from downtown singles to tourists with kids in tow, and the Disneyesque interior—with its open kitchen, spearlike fish grill and glittery lights—has enough dazzle for them all. The menu adds glitzy spins to New England seafood in such dishes as spit-roasted sword-fish with Maine crab vinaigrette, miso-marinated sea bass, and crispy lobster with ginger and scallions, and updates the traditional surf-and-turf (steak paired with lobster tail) with a chipotle marinade. Adventurous fish aficionados go for the raw bar and the selection of ceviche.

Mamma Maria $$$ Italian

3 North Square, North End. Dinner only. 617-523-0077. www.mammamaria.com.

Dine here to enjoy neo-Italian food that isn't too, too nouveau. They do fish, braised meats and pasta with equal flair; think homemade spinach spaghet-tini tossed with Maine shrimp, roasted garlic and local sweet corn (fabulous!) and hand-rolled pap-pardelle with rabbit, pancetta and rosemary. Lots of places come and go in the North End, but this one has stuck around and continues to make fans of first-time diners.

Olives $$$ Mediterranean

10 City Square, Charlestown. Dinner only. 617-242-1999. www.toddenglish.com.

A communal farmhouse table forms the centerpiece of the rustic dining room where chef Todd English's staff prepares memorable meals in the open kitchen. Classic picks in the award-winning restaurant include wood-grilled chunks of squid and octopus in a chickpea, tomato and toasted-garlic vinaigrette; grilled duck breast in maple marinade; hand-crafted pastas; and vanilla-bean soufflé.

Sage $$$ New Italian

69 Prince St., North End. Dinner only. Closed Sun. 617-248-8814. www.sageboston.com.

A small dining room, a tiny kitchen and an ambitious menu—somehow, owner/ chef Anthony Susi makes it work at this gem of a restaurant in the North End, Boston's Little Italy. The cuisine is Italian, of course, but of a newer vintage, with plenty of goat cheese, artichokes, beets and fine Italian spices standing in for bland red sauce. The hand-rolled potato gnocchi is a favorite.

Sonsie $$$ New American

327 Newbury St., Back Bay. 617-351-2500. www.sonsieboston.com.

High-rent Newbury Street, with its profusion of designer boutiques, sports a number of cafes and outdoor eateries, but none is more popular or ingeniously versatile than Sonsie. In the morning, white-aproned staff glide between the marble tables and wicker chairs to deliver espressos, cappuccinos and croissants, while lunchtime pastas, grilled sandwiches and brick-oven pizzas provide the fuel needed for the day's shopping splurge. Dinner can be either casual in the cafe, where the floor-to-ceiling windows (folded back in summer) provide ample opportunities for people-watching, or more intimate in the restaurant, with its cozy booths, linen tablecloths and Mediterranean décor. And in true European style, the well-appointed bar serves everything from macchiatos to martinis all day long.

Teatro $$$ Italian

177 Tremont St., Downtown. Dinner only. 617-778-6841. www.teatroboston.com.

Set inside a former synagogue, with 15-foot arched ceilings, this Theater District hot spot is lovely to look at, but noisy as all get out. Forget the quiet conversation and join the young, hip crowd for hearty rustic Italian fare, featuring tasty fresh pasta and excellent antipasti. The veal saltimbocca with creamed spinach and mushrooms is an artful blend of crispy and creamy—don't miss it.

Tremont 647 $$$ New American

647 Tremont St., South End. Dinner & Sun. brunch only. 617-266-4600. www.tremont647.com.

Chef Andy Husbands borrows flavors from around the globe to create "adventurous cuisine" such as pork-filled momo dumplings, and sea bass wrapped in a banana leaf. Art Deco chandeliers shaped like calla lily bouquets decorate the small South End dining room that draws a hip, must-wear-black crowd. The Sunday pajama brunch, when both staff and patrons show up in their nightclothes, is the next best thing to breakfast in bed.

Union Oyster House
$$$ Seafood

41 Union St., Downtown. 617-227-2750. www.unionoysterhouse.com.

JFK slurped oysters here, at the oldest restaurant in Boston (1826). You'll go for the historic appeal, but you'll fall for the pub-like atmosphere and food that's better than you'd expect. Grab a seat at the raw bar for a true Boston experience.

Inexpensive

East Coast Grill & Raw Bar
$$ American

1271 Cambridge St., Cambridge. Dinner & Sun brunch only. 617-491-6568. www.eastcoastgrill.net.

"Grills just want to have fun" is the theme at this Inman Square landmark, where crowds still gather for fresh grilled fish paired with tropical fruit salsas, and southern-style barbecue. Chris Schlesinger's pulled-pork sandwiches are a messy plateful of heaven. Casual and loud, it's cool for a crowd, but the dishes pack plenty of heat, especially on "Hell Nights" when area chile lovers gather to test their mettle (even the pasta is hellishly hot).

Finale
$$ Desserts

One Columbus Ave., Back Bay; 617-423-3184. Also at Harvard Square, 30 Dunster St., Cambridge; 617-441-9797. www.finaledesserts.com.

Got a serious sweet tooth? Make tracks to this swanky dessert cafe, where the Theater District meets Back Bay. Sandwiches and light meals are available, but the real reason to stop here is for the decadent, if pricey, desserts. Molten chocolate cakes with warm, gooey centers are a real crowd pleaser, as is the classic crème brûlée. If you're a true chocoholic (with deep pockets), order the Chocolate Obsession, an orgy of a tasting plate, for two.

Giacomo's
$$ Italian

355 Hanover St., North End; 617-523-9026. Dinner only. Also at 431 Columbus Ave., South End; 617-536-5723.

If you're craving platters full of red sauce and pasta, grab a table at this perennial favorite. The casual, cash-only restaurant serves up simple, hearty fare at decent prices. The fried calamari with marinara sauce will warm your bones on a cold Boston night, and the salmon and sun-dried tomatoes in tomato cream sauce over fettucine is every bit as good as it sounds.

Ginza
$$ Japanese

16 Hudson St., Chinatown. Other locations in Brookline and Watertown. Open until 2am nightly. 617-338-2261.

Tucked away in Chinatown, Ginza serves up top-quality sushi and sashimi. The menu includes Japanese standards, from tempura to teriyaki to sukiyaki, but the raw fish is the main catch here. Look for the unusual maki rolls, like the B-52 roll (yellowtail layered with tempura) or the shaped-like-its-name caterpillar maki. Traditional low tables in the back room, where you sit on pillows on the floor, are quieter than the standard seating in the busy front room.

Legal Sea Foods $$ Seafood

26 Park Plaza, Back Bay. Check online for other locations throughout the Boston area.
617-426-4444. www.legalseafoods.com.

With branches around the city, this seafood chain has been a local favorite for
more than 40 years. The Park Square location is the flagship. Legal Sea Foods serves
some 20 varieties of fish each day, in a
fresh, straightforward manner. A few menu
items have an Asian edge, like the tasty
steamed mussels in a fragrant seafood
broth. The thickly-cut French fries are
outstanding, as is the clam chowder, served in both calorie-dense creamy, and
light preparations. Whichever way you go, you won't be disappointed.

New Shanghai $$ Chinese

21 Hudson St., Chinatown. 617-338-6699.

Most restaurants in Boston's Chinatown serve Cantonese-style dishes, but New
Shanghai specializes in Shanghai-style fare. The crispy scallops with black-
pepper sauce, the pan-fried rice cakes (thick oval noodles sautéed with meat,
seafood or vegetables) and the exotic braised eel are all good choices. Pastel
tablecloths, lacquered chairs and tropical fish tanks distinguish New Shanghai
from the neighborhood's generally modest eateries.

No Name Restaurant $$ Seafood

15 ½ Fish Pier, off Northern Ave., South Boston. 617-338-7539.

No name and no nonsense—and no credit cards—this simple fish house near
the World Trade Center is a favorite of in-the-know locals who don't mind that
the service is rather gruff—it's all about the food here. You may luck into a table
in the back with a harbor view; if you don't, you'll sit family-style and enjoy the
perfect seafood chowder and platters of fish, served broiled or fried.

Mr. Bartley's Burger Cottage $ American

1246 Massachusetts Ave., Cambridge. Closed Sun. 617-354-6559. www.mrbartleys.com.

If you're looking for organic or fusion cuisine,
go elsewhere, since it's the thick, juicy ham-
burgers, paired with crisp onion rings or sweet-
potato fries, that entice crowds of students,
locals and tourists to this bustling Harvard
Square institution. Since 1961, they've offered a
menu of "wicked ahhsome" burgers and fabulous frappes (that's milkshake, to you out-of-
towners) and lime rickeys. Vintage posters and
cramped wooden tables give the room a de-
cided 1960s feel. Be sure to bring cash; Mr.
Bartley's doesn't accept credit cards.

The Paramount $ American

14 Charles St., Beacon Hill. 617-720-1132.

There's nothing stuffy about this Beacon Hill landmark, a popular cafeteria-style restaurant with decent food and easy-on-the-pocketbook prices. This is where locals—and visitors in the know—head for hefty plates of bacon and eggs and steaming buttermilk pancakes in the morning, or freshly made sandwiches at lunchtime. Evenings, the tiny room turns intimate, with low lights, piped-in jazz and table service. Serving three meals a day, seven days a week, The Paramount is one of the few affordable places left on the Hill.

Pho Pasteur $ Vietnamese

119 Newbury St., Back Bay. Other locations in Cambridge, Chestnut Hill and Allston. 617-262-8200.

Is it possible to eat on the cheap on trendy Newbury Street? Absolutely. You won't do much better than Pho Pasteur, where the big, steaming bowls of noodle soup will cure whatever ails you. The eaterie also offers a selection of other light and tasty dishes made with beef, chicken, pork, tofu and veggies.

Sultan's Kitchen $ Turkish

72 Broad St., Downtown. Closed Sun. No dinner Sat. 617-728-2828.

A modest take-out spot with just a handful of tables, this tiny Turkish eatery is an excellent option for vegetarians or anyone looking for a fast, flavorful meal in the Financial District. The speedy staff will pack your choices to go, if you prefer to picnic at the waterfront, just a short walk away. Middle Eastern salads and sandwiches, including several types of kebabs, are featured, but be sure to leave room for a piece of the delightfully syrupy baklava.

Warren Tavern $ American

2 Pleasant St., Charlestown. 617-241-8142. www.warrentavern.com.

With its low timbered ceilings, snug fireplace and long mahogany bar, this tavern may resemble an English pub, but in fact it's just as American as they come—Patriot, that is. Constructed c.1780, the structure was one of the first to be rebuilt after the British torched Charlestown in 1775. Doubling as a Masonic hall, the alehouse was a favorite of Paul Revere (whether the juicy Paul Revere Burger with sautéed mushrooms and Swiss has anything to do with the silversmith's culinary preferences is uncertain). George Washington was known to quaff a few here, too. Today Warren Tavern remains a cozy place for a cold Sam Adams beer and shepherd's pie (a house specialty), or hot chocolate by the fire, after a long day on the Freedom Trail.

Dining on Cape Cod, Martha's Vineyard and Nantucket

Restaurants listed in this section are open year-round unless otherwise noted.

Luxury

The Pearl $$$$ Asian-fusion

12 Federal St., Nantucket. Dinner only. Closed Dec–Apr. 508-228-9701.
www.boardinghouse-pearl.com.

Lavish and exotic, the Asian-fusion dishes at this tony hot spot are as wildly inventive as the tropical fish in the dining room's sparkling aquarium are luminous. From the

yellowfin-tuna martini to the salt-and-pepper lobster with Asian barbecue sauce to the sauté of prawns and sweetbreads served with sweet-potato mousse and beet greens, the Pearl packs plenty of excitement onto its plates. The young, the adventurous, and the trust-fund-endowed are all here, making it a scene with a capital S.

Sweet Life Café $$$$ New American

63 Circuit Ave., Oak Bluffs, Martha's Vineyard. Dinner only. Closed Dec–Mar. 508-696-0200.

Choose a candlelit table inside this warm Victorian house, whose romantic ambience lies worlds away from the hustle-bustle of Oak Bluffs. If the weather is fine, sit outside in the garden, which is lit by twinkling white lights. Inside or out, such New American dishes as pan-roasted halibut with eggplant purée and curried onion rings are definitely worth a trip.

Moderate

Alchemy $$$ New French

71 Main St., Edgartown, Martha's Vineyard. Call for winter hours. 508-627-9999.
White walls and white-cloth-topped tables form the backdrop for the colorful French-inspired cuisine at this smartly casual two-level Edgartown bistro. Dinner

entrées run the gamut from pan-roasted cod to lobster risotto to sirloin paired with "cheesy fondue;" the lighter bar menu offers salmon cakes, Cuban sandwiches, and tequila-and-lime-glazed chicken. The curved, polished-wood bar draws year-'rounders and vacationers alike.

Cape Sea Grille $$$ Seafood

31 Sea St., Harwich Port, Cape Cod. Dinner only. Closed Nov–mid-Apr. 508-432-4745.
www.capeseagrille.com.

You don't have to love fish to eat here, but if you do, the contemporary seafood dishes are definitely worth a detour to Harwich Port. Filling an old sea captain's house, the dining rooms—with white tablecloths and captain's chairs—are not spacious. Better to focus on the food: seafood paella with clams, shrimp and chorizo; crispy seafood piccata with capers and olives; or halibut in an Asian-inspired coconut-milk sauce. The warm chocolate truffle cake makes a decadent finale.

Centre Street Bistro

$$$ New American

9 Centre St., Nantucket. 508-228-8470. www.nantucketbistro.com.

Inventive food, a casual atmosphere, and moderate prices (for Nantucket) make this diminutive bistro worth a visit. The tiny dining room, with cheery yellow walls and floral-cushioned chairs, is a tight squeeze, but in mild weather you can sit outside on the patio. At lunch they offer intriguing salads, as well as new twists on old favorites, like a BLT with parmesan aioli. Dinner follows the same contemporary direction: seared-scallop Napoleon is a visual delight, with layers of scallops and thick slabs of tomato, avocado and herbs, sandwiched between squares of fried tortilla. Be sure to bring cash; Centre Street doesn't take credit cards.

Sconset Café

$$$ New American

Post Office Square, Siasconset, Nantucket. Closed mid-Oct–mid-May. 508-257-4008. www.sconsetcafe.com.

In a simply-turned-out storefront on the island's east end, this contemporary cafe makes a relaxed spot for a breakfast, lunch or dinner, far from the bustle of Nantucket village. The lunch menu features updated versions of classic sandwiches and salads; in the evenings, fare runs to such dishes as crab cakes remoulade (a specialty here), and sautéed halibut finished with a coconut-curry rub, served with basmati rice. Don't expect private conversation here, though; the tables are nearly on top of one another!

Sfoglia

$$$ Italian

130 Pleasant St., Nantucket. Dinner only. Closed Sun. Call for winter hours. 508-325-4500. www.sfogliarestaurant.com.

There's serious cooking going on in this mid-island house with its mismatched wooden tables and chairs and eclectic assortment of crockery. The menu of modern Italian regional cuisine may be small, but husband-and-wife chef/owners Ron Suhanosky and Colleen Marnell-Suhanosky are unquestionably talented. Pastas are handmade (the potato gnocchi, served with roasted cauliflower in scrumptious clove cream, seem lighter than air) and desserts are dynamite.

Inexpensive

The Flume

$$ New England

13 Lake Ave. off Rte. 130, Mashpee, Cape Cod. Dinner only. Closed late Nov–mid-Apr. 508-477-1456.

This modest house, nestled among the pines, may be nothing special to look at, but if you're hankering for old-fashioned New England cookery, it may be just the place. Owned by Wampanoag elder Earl Mills Sr., it serves such local classics as Yankee pot roast, chicken pot pie, and plenty of seafood, including broiled scrod, lobster Newburg, and fried smelts. Depending on the season, you might find shad roe or soft-shelled crab. Roast turkey dinner is the favorite Sunday special.

Fog Island Cafe
$$ New American

*7 S. Water St., Nantucket. Breakfast & lunch year-round; dinner Jun–Labor Day.
508-228-1818. www.fogisland.com.*

On Nantucket, even down-home is relatively upscale: witness this inviting cafe, with sturdy wooden tables, where owners Mark and Anne Dawson, graduates of the Culinary Institute of America, serve up American comfort food with a contemporary edge. Throughout the year, it's a popular spot for breakfast (eggs, pancakes, breakfast sandwiches) and lunch (soups, burgers, wraps); in summer, the cafe offers moderately priced American fare in the evenings as well.

Art Cliff Diner
$ American

39 Beach Rd., Vineyard Haven, Martha's Vineyard. Closed Wed. 508-693-1224.

Although the open rafters and old-fashioned blue-and-white-checkered tablecloths would steer you to order plain old bacon and eggs or a burger and fries here, this diner's fare shows an innovative touch. Eggs might come in a chorizo frittata, waffles might be pumpkin-flavored, and lunch options encompass crispy fish tacos, grilled-eggplant sandwiches, and an asparagus-prosciutto salad.

Cap'n Frosty's
$ Seafood

219 Main St. (Rte. 6A), Dennis, Cape Cod. Closed Labor Day–Mar. 508-385-8548.

Fried seafood is a Cape specialty, and this Dennis clam shack does a good job with crispy-battered clams, scallops and other delicacies of the deep. Place your order at the counter, and then hunt for a seat at one of the Formica-topped tables in the bare-bones dining room. It's not a place to linger—there's no ambience and it's generally packed—but you can bring the kids and not worry about tracking in sand! Nobody passes up ice cream for dessert.

Pie in the Sky Bakery
$ American

10 Water St., Woods Hole, Cape Cod. 508-540-5475. www.woodshole.com/pie.

Woods Hole residents are up and about early, between the marine center's activity and the constant arrival and departure of the Martha's Vineyard ferries at the Steamship Authority. So buy a newspaper and head for this pleasant cafe for coffee and breakfast fare. Espresso, cappuccino, fresh-baked muffins and pastries are served beginning at 7am (8am Sun); sandwiches and salads are available for lunch and dinner. Sit inside or out on the little patio.

Another Way to Look at It: Restaurants by Theme

Looking for a restaurant with outdoor dining or a place to take the kids? In the preceding pages, we've organized the eateries by price category, so below we've broken them out by theme to help you plan your meals while you're in town. *Restaurants are located in Boston, unless otherwise noted.*

Breakfast Spots
Art Cliff Diner (Martha's Vineyard) *(p 112)*
Fog Island Cafe (Nantucket) *(p 112)*
The Paramount *(p 109)*
Pie in the Sky Bakery (Cape Cod) *(p 112)*
Sconset Café (Nantucket) *(p 111)*

Easy on the Budget
Art Cliff Diner (Martha's Vineyard) *(p 112)*
The Flume (Cape Cod) *(p 111)*
Mr. Bartley's Burger Cottage
   (Cambridge) *(p 108)*
The Paramount *(p 109)*
Pho Pasteur *(p 109)*
Pie in the Sky Bakery (Cape Cod) *(p 112)*

Ethnic Experiences
Ginza *(p 107)*
Mantra *(p 103)*
New Shanghai *(p 108)*
Sultan's Kitchen *(p 109)*

Neighborhood Favorites
Alchemy *(p 110)*
Cap'n Frosty's (Cape Cod) *(p 112)*
Giacomo's *(p 107)*
Hamersley's Bistro *(p 103)*
Harvest (Cambridge) *(p 104)*
No Name Restaurant *(p 108)*
Sage *(p 106)*
Sfoglia (Nantucket) *(p 111)*
Warren Tavern (Charlestown) *(p 109)*

Outdoor Dining
Centre Street Bistro *(p 111)*
Hamersley's Bistro *(p 103)*
Pie in the Sky Bakery (Cape Cod) *(p 112)*
Sonsie *(p 106)*
Sweet Life Café (Martha's Vineyard) *(p 110)*

Places to Eat with Kids
Cap'n Frosty's (Cape Cod) *(p 112)*
Durgin-Park *(p 104)*

Fog Island Cafe (Nantucket) *(p 112)*
Jasper White's Summer Shack *(p 105)*
Kingfish Hall *(p 105)*

Power Lunch Spots
Grill 23 & Bar *(p 103)*
Radius *(p 104)*

Pre- and Post-theater Dining
Finale *(p 107)*
Teatro *(p 106)*

Restaurants near Shopping
Legal Sea Foods *(p 108)*
Pho Pasteur *(p 109)*
Sonsie *(p 106)*

Restaurants with History
Durgin-Park *(p 104)*
Mamma Maria *(p 105)*
Union Oyster House *(p 107)*
Warren Tavern (Charlestown) *(p 109)*

Seafood
Cape Sea Grille (Cape Cod) *(p 110)*
Great Bay *(p 102)*
Jasper White's Summer Shack *(p 105)*
Kingfish Hall *(p 105)*
Legal Sea Foods *(p 108)*
The Pearl *(p 110)*

Star Chefs
Great Bay (Michael Schlow) *(p 102)*
Jasper White's Summer Shack (Jasper
   White) *(p 105)*
Kingfish Hall (Todd English) *(p 105)*
Olives (Todd English) *(p 105)*
Rialto (Jody Adams) (Cambridge) *(p 104)*
Tremont 647 (Andy Husbands) *(p 106)*

Sunday Brunch
Aujourd'hui *(p 102)*
East Coast Grill & Raw Bar
   (Cambridge) *(p 107)*
Tremont 647 *(p 106)*

Must Stay: Boston Area Hotels

The properties listed below were selected for their ambience, location and/or value for money. Prices reflect the average cost for a standard double room for two people in high season. High season in Boston is summer and fall (Jun–Oct); rates in Boston are usually lower in spring and winter. Many hotels on Cape Cod, Martha's Vineyard and Nantucket close in the winter months. Price ranges quoted do not reflect the Boston hotel tax of 12.45% or the 9.7% state lodging tax on Cape Cod and the islands. For a selected listing of lodgings by theme (Hotels with History, Posh Places, etc.), see p 125. Properties in this section are located in Boston unless otherwise noted.

$$$$$	Over $350	**$$**	$100–$175
$$$$	$250–$350	**$**	Under $100
$$$	$175–$250		

Luxury

Four Seasons Hotel Boston $$$$$ 272 rooms

200 Boylston St., Back Bay. 617-338-4400 or 800-332-3442. www.fourseasons.com.

This elegant grand dame, set above the Public Garden, has been a favorite of well-heeled business and pleasure travelers for more than 20 years. Attentive service is its hallmark, along with generous on-site amenities like 24-hour room service, free shoe shines and complimentary town car drop-off service. Considered one of the top hotels in the world, the Four Seasons offers well-appointed rooms, updated with luxurious fabrics, flat-screen TVs and high-speed Internet access. Splurge on a dinner in the hotel's award-winning **Aujourd'hui** restaurant *(see Must Eat)*, one of the city's best.

Ritz-Carlton $$$$$ 326 rooms

15 Arlington St., Back Bay. 617-536-5700 or 800-241-3333. www.ritzcarlton.com.

The oldest Ritz-Carlton hotel in continuous operation in the US is a Boston landmark. Overlooking the Public Garden, the lavish property, filled with original art, rich fabrics and glittering chandeliers, is known for its over-the-top luxury and impeccable service. A recent $60 million renovation spruced up the venerable hotel and added high-tech touches. It's the traditional place to stay in Boston, if money is no object.

Ritz-Carlton Boston Common $$$$$ 193 rooms

10 Avery St., Beacon Hill. 617-574-7100 or 800-241-3333. www.ritzcarlton.com.

Prefer modern art to Old World antiques? Consider the new Ritz Carlton, with a convenient location on Boston Common. This contemporary glass-and-brick monolith boasts a $1 million modern art collection, sleek furnishings and legendary Ritz-style service. Guests have access to an adjacent spa, fitness and sports facility. This Ritz property is a magnet for international travelers.

Westin Copley Place $$$$$ 800 rooms

10 Huntington Ave., Copley Place, Back Bay. 617-262-9600 or 888-625-5144. www.starwoodhotels.com/westin.

This gleaming glass-and-steel high rise sits in busy Copley Place with skywalk access to Copley Place and Prudential Center shops. The 36-story hotel draws hordes of business travelers and convention-eers who like the Back Bay location and can afford the hefty prices. Rooms are done in earth tones with comfy beds and Starbucks coffee for in-rooms coffeepots. Ask about package deals.

XV Beacon $$$$$ 63 rooms

15 Beacon St., Beacon Hill. 617-670-1500 or 877-982-3226. www.xvbeacon.com.

Unsurpassed luxury is what you'll find at this Beacon Hill hotel. The Beaux-Arts building's original 1903 cage elevator whisks guests up to oversized rooms outfitted with canopy beds, gas fireplaces and mahogany paneling. Amenities include person-alized business cards and in-room gadgets like four-inch LCD TVs in the bathroom and a printer/scanner/fax machine. **The Federalist ($$$$)** restaurant serves contem-porary French cuisine under silver chandeliers in an elegant beige dining room.

Boston Harbor Hotel $$$$ 229 rooms

70 Rowes Wharf, Waterfront. 617-439-7000 or 800-752-7077. www.bhh.com.

Overlooking Boston Harbor, this grand hotel—located across from the Financial District—boasts some of the city's best water views. Chandeliers, marble floors and plush furnishings add classical elegance. Spacious rooms feature marble baths and nightly turndown service. The **Meritage ($$$)** restaurant, with windows facing the water, showcases contemporary New England cuisine, wine pairings and small plates.

Must Stay: Boston Area Hotels

Boston Marriott Long Wharf $$$$ 408 rooms

296 State St., Waterfront. 617-227-0800 or 800-228-9290.
www.marriott.com/propertypage/BOSLW.

Its waterfront location, popular after-work bars, a public walkway and an open lobby make this large hotel a lively, integral part of the city's seaside scene. Most guest rooms have water views, and the property boasts a nice indoor pool and health club. It's super-convenient to waterfront attractions like the Boston Aquarium, Faneuil Hall and Boston Harbor boat trips and water taxis.

Charles Hotel $$$$ 337 rooms

1 Bennett St., Cambridge. 617-864-1200 or 800-882-1818. www.charleshotel.com.

Within walking distance of Harvard Square, this contemporary luxury hotel is a longtime favorite of Cambridge visitors. The modern exterior looks like a jumble of square and rectangular blocks, but in the traditional red brick that echoes the Harvard campus. Inside, you'll find bright and airy rooms, simple four-poster beds and Shaker-style furniture. Bright quilts and paintings add colorful accents. Dinner in top-ranked **Rialto** *(see Must Eat)* is a must, and the **Regattabar** is a top haunt for jazz lovers *(see p 79)*. Guests can rejuvenate next door at Le Pli Spa *(see Must Be Pampered)* or work out at the adjacent health club.

Fairmont Copley Plaza Hotel $$$$ 383 rooms

138 St. James Ave., Back Bay. 617-267-5300 or 800-257-7544. www.fairmont.com/copleyplaza.

Glamour, gold and glitz are the operative words at the Fairmont. Back Bay's palatial property has been the home base for visiting US presidents and foreign dignitaries since 1912. A look at the lobby's gilded coffered ceilings, crystal chandeliers and ornate French Renaissance-style furnishings may explain why Elizabeth Taylor and Richard Burton spent their second honeymoon here. The dark paneled ornate **Oak Bar** is a favorite spot for drinks, boasting one of the largest martini menus in town.

Hotel Marlowe $$$$ 236 rooms

25 Edwin H. Land Blvd., Cambridge. 617-868-8000 or 800-825-7140. www.hotelmarlowe.com.

This boutique hotel, across the river in Cambridge and minutes from Harvard and MIT, brims with bold colors and whimsical touches. Animal-print carpeting meets gold and red-velvet fabrics and striped furniture in this lively venue. Rooms are spacious and a bit more soothing than the public areas, with neutral colors punctuated with colorful splashes. They have plenty of modern conveniences and amenities, like Frette bed linens, high-speed Internet access and CD stereos. The nightly complimentary wine hour, held in the small lobby area, is a hit with guests.

urys Boston Hotel $$$$ 223 rooms

50 Stuart St., Back Bay. 617-266-7200. www.jurysdoyle.com/boston-hotel.

Part of Ireland's premier hotel group, this new property in Back Bay is located in the historic 1920s Boston Police Headquarters building. If the idea of sleeping in a former jail doesn't intrigue you, the sophisticated and luxurious atmosphere may. Old World charm meets New with a simple, almost serene, décor of neutral palettes, dark woods and traditional furnishings. Ambience is friendly and casual, with an at-the-ready staff to help you. On-site **Stanhope ($$$)** restaurant and **Cuffs** Irish bar are popular with locals and visitors alike.

angham Hotel $$$$ 325 rooms

250 Franklin St., Downtown. 617-451-1900 or 800-543-4300. www.langhamhotels.com/langham/boston.

Built in the 1920s to house the Federal Reserve Bank of Boston, this dignified granite-and-limestone structure in the Financial District now houses a luxury hotel (formerly Le Meridien.) Well-appointed rooms (with large lighted closets, plush robes, make-up mirrors) possess distinctive features such as dramatic sloping windows with sweeping city, park or courtyard views. **ulien ($$$)**, the hotel's formal restaurant, serves contemporary French fare. More casual **Café Fleuri ($$)** hosts the popular Chocolate Bar, an all-you-can-eat chocolate extravaganza *(Sat, Sept–June)*. Popular with business travelers during the week, the Langham periodically offers weekend specials.

enox Hotel $$$$ 213 rooms

61 Exeter St. at Boylston St., Back Bay. 617-536-5300 or 800-225-7676. www.lenoxhotel.com.

A Boston landmark, this historic property has been serving Boston dignitaries, celebrities and visitors since 1900. The property has been family-owned since 1963 and prides itself on over-the-top service. The hotel was beautifully restored in 2003; now the public areas and rooms gleam with deep jewel colors, dark woods, rich tapestries and rugs, and crystal and brass accents. Some corner rooms have wood-burning fireplaces; other rooms boast views of Back Bay and the Charles River. Its location, within walking distance of Newbury Street shops and restaurants, is an added plus.

Nine Zero $$$$ 190 rooms

90 Tremont St., Downtown. 617-772-5800. www.ninezero.com.

One of Boston's finest boutique-style hotels, this sleek and stylish property, just off Boston Common, is a favorite among travelers looking for quiet, upscale lodgings. The redbrick-and-limestone facade is Old Boston, but inside you'll find a contemporary space, with plenty of glass, nickel, chrome and steel. The effect is serene; sink into fresh Frette linens, pull up the goose-down comforter and turn on the music. The hotel's restaurant, **Spire ($$$)**, is considered one of the best in the city.

Onyx Hotel
$$$$ 112 rooms

155 Portland St., Downtown. 617-557-9955. www.onyxhotel.com.

Arty, splashy and sexy describe this new boutique hotel, located in Boston's revitalized Bullfinch Triangle, three blocks from bustling North Station. You'll be dazzled by the first thing you'll see: the luscious Ruby Room, with its curvy lines, deep-red fabrics, and black-granite bar (with fiber optics to make your drinks twinkle!). The flash—think black and white and red splashes of color against a neutral taupe backdrop—continues throughout the tiny lobby and good-sized rooms.

Seaport Hotel
$$$$ 437 rooms

One Seaport Lane, South Boston. 617-385-4000 or 877-732-7678. www.seaportboston.com

This soaring high rise, next to the Seaport World Trade Center, is a magnet for conventioneers and business travelers. Rooms are spacious; some offer sweeping views of Boston Harbor or the city skyline. The on-site health and fitness center, with spa services, is a nice amenity. Families who don't mind staying a bit out of town (bus service is now available to South Station) will enjoy the large indoor pool, in-room movies and video games, and children's menu at the award-wining **Aura ($$$$)** restaurant.

Moderate

Beacon Hill Hotel and Bistro
$$$ 13 rooms

25 Charles St., Beacon Hill. 617-723-7575 or 888-959-2442. www.beaconhillhotel.com.

If the weather is mild, slip up to the roof terrace at this swank small hotel on Beacon Hill's main street to sip a glass of wine and watch the world go by. Like the terrace, the entire property feels like a stylish urban oasis. Rooms are sleek, almost spare, sporting fluffy duvets and hi-tech flat-screen TVs. Rates include a full breakfast in the Parisian-style bistro, which also serves high-quality French cuisine at lunch and dinner.

A Cambridge House, Bed and Breakfast Inn
$$$ 15 rooms

2218 Massachusetts Ave., Cambridge. 617-491-6300 or 800-232-9989.
www.acambridgehouse.com.

This immaculately decorated turn-of-the-19C Victorian is filled with rich fabrics, plush area rugs and fine antiques. The romantic rooms are elegant and spacious, most with working fireplaces, all with private baths, high-speed Internet access and cable TV. Although it's located on busy Massachusetts Avenue, minutes from Harvard Square, the house sits back from the road, and once inside, it's nice and quiet. A large breakfast buffet is served each morning.

Clarendon Square Inn $$$ 3 rooms

198 W. Brookline St., South End. 617-536-2229. www.clarendonsquare.com.

Not your grandmother's B&B, this South End brownstone is stylishly appointed with a mix of Victorian antiques and contemporary designer touches. Modern art adorns the parlor walls, and marble mantels surround the fireplaces. Hotel-style amenities—voice-mail service, hair dryers, a guest refrigerator—abound, and continental breakfast is served in the sunshine-yellow dining room. You can soak away the stresses of the day in the hot tub up on the rooftop deck.

Eliot Hotel $$$ 95 rooms

370 Commonwealth Ave., Back Bay. 617-267-1607 or 800-443-5468. www.eliothotel.com.

One of Back Bay's best values, this quiet, European-style boutique hotel, overlooking pretty Commonwealth Avenue, features spacious suites, with living room, bedroom and kitchenette. French doors separate the bedroom from the living area, and antiques and floral fabrics decorate the spaces. Marble baths, antique reproductions, and amenities like cozy robes, fine cotton bed linens, Internet access and 24-hour room service add to the opulence. The on-site, award-winning **Clio ($$$$)** restaurant is a favorite dining spot among Bostonians, as is **Uni**, the Eliot's new sashimi bar and lounge.

Hotel @ MIT $$$ 210 rooms

20 Sidney St., Cambridge. 617-577-0200. www.univparkhotel.com.

What would you expect from the brainy, high-tech folks at the renowned Massachusetts Institute of Technology? Exactly this! The ultra-contemporary hotel, located near Central Square in Cambridge, is playful and eclectic, with moving sculptures, robots from the MIT Artificial Intelligence Lab, exposed circuitry, neon lights, and original artwork from the MIT collection. High-tech features and toys are found throughout the hotel. Pull up an ergonomically designed chair, and enjoy! This is surely one of the most interesting places to stay in the area.

Hotel Commonwealth $$$ 150 rooms

500 Commonwealth Ave., Back Bay. 617-933-5000 or 866-784-4000. www.hotelcommonwealth.com.

One of Boston's newest properties, this independently owned luxury hotel sits at once-seedy Kenmore Square, within a ball's pitch to legendary Fenway Park. There are two styles of rooms, one with a view of Fenway (popular with zealous Red Sox fans) featuring a small sitting area; the other is slightly larger (an additional 30 square feet) with views of Commonwealth Avenue. All have writing desks, marble baths, flat-screen TVs, DVD players, and high-speed Internet access. A meal in the hotel's **Great Bay** restaurant *(see Must Eat)* is a highlight.

Millennium Bostonian Hotel
$$$ 201 rooms

26 North St. at Faneuil Hall, Downtown. 617-523-3600. www.millenium-hotels.com.

If you like to be in the middle of the action, you can't beat this European-style hotel at bustling Faneuil Hall Marketplace. A stunning steel sculpture and a fountain greet guests at the cobblestone rotary outside the check-in area; the lobby sits beneath a soaring atrium of glass and steel. Rooms in the older wing, a converted 1824 warehouse, feature high ceilings, tall windows, wooden beams, exposed brick walls and working fireplaces. New-wing rooms sport a sleek design with wood paneling, and warm red and yellow accents. Some rooms have balconies overlooking Faneuil Hall or the North End. The full-service Aveda Salon and Spa and the award-winning **Seasons ($$$)** restaurant are on-site.

Omni Parker House
$$$ 551 rooms

60 School St., Downtown. 617-227-8600 or 800-843-6664. www.omnihotels.com.

A Boston landmark and the oldest continuously operating hotel in the country, the Omni faces Boston Common at the foot of Beacon Hill. Expect hushed, Brahmin-style elegance: wood-paneled walls, jeweled-colored fabrics, brass elevator doors, low lights and cherry furniture. This is where young upstart John F. Kennedy announced his first campaign for public office; the hotel continues to draw visiting politicians and businesspeople. Rooms are smallish but comfortable, and updated with modern, high-tech conveniences.

Inexpensive

Chandler Inn Hotel
$$ 56 rooms

26 Chandler St., South End. 617-482-3450 or 800-842-3450. www.chandlerinn.com.

You'll get great value at this casual, friendly hotel in the lively, revitalized South End. The eight-story high rise is within walking distance of Back Bay shopping and dining, and an easy subway ride to citywide attractions. Rooms are simply furnished, with double or twin beds, TVs, Internet access, and come with complimentary continental breakfast. A two-night minimum stay is required during summer weekends.

Encore
$$ 3 rooms

116 West Newton St., South End. 617-247-3425. www.encorebandb.com.

A quiet alternative to large convention hotels, this small, classy B&B in the now-trendy South End has three individually decorated guest rooms. Natural light abounds in the contemporary-style rooms, each with private bath and queen-size bed. Design is sleek, with brick accent walls, wood beams, and streamlined furnishings done in shades of green, brown and purple. A stay at the renovated 19C town house also includes continental breakfast—and Boston skyline views.

Harborside Inn $$ 54 rooms

185 State St., Waterfront. 617-723-7500 or 888-723-7565. www.harborsideinnboston.com.

Looking for a great location, a historic property and a good value? Check out this hotel in the Financial District, steps from Faneuil Hall, Quincy Marketplace and the waterfront. Rooms in this converted 1858 mercantile warehouse are individually decorated, featuring exposed granite-and-brick walls, polished wood floors, high ceilings, sleigh beds and authentic Oriental rugs.

John Jeffries House $$ 46 rooms

14 David G. Mugar Way at Charles Circle, Beacon Hill. 617-367-1866. www.johnjeffrieshouse.com.

At the foot of Beacon Hill, this solid-looking four-story redbrick building, built in the early 1900s, sits opposite a bustling traffic circle and the Charles Street T station. Despite its location, the inside is surprisingly serene. Well-maintained rooms are furnished with period reproductions, and most have kitchen facilities. Although the guest rooms are not large, many have separate sitting areas. Enjoy a continental breakfast in the large parlor, which offers oversize chairs and views of the Charles River.

Newbury Guest House $$ 32 rooms

261 Newbury St., Back Bay. 617-437-7666 or 800-437-7668. www.newburyguesthouse.com.

Set on Boston's prime shopping street, this guest house, comprising three attached 1880s brownstones, is an excellent value for the neighborhood. It's close enough to the Hynes Convention Center and the many Back Bay corporate offices to draw both business travelers and vacationers. Rooms, some with bay windows, are furnished with Victorian-style reproductions and Oriental rugs. A continental breakfast is served in the petite parlor.

Wyndham Boston $$ 428 rooms

89 Broad St., Downtown. 617-556-0006 or 877-999-3223. www.wyndham.com.

You can't beat the location of this luxury chain hotel near popular Faneuil Hall and the waterfront, or its value pricing. Rooms at this high-rise property are standard issue, with décor that is a combination of Art Deco brick, brass and woods, ensconced in earth tones. Amenities include plush bathrobes, high-speed Internet access, and Sony Playstations for the kids (big and small).

Copley Inn $ 21 rooms

19 Garrison St., Back Bay. 617-236-0300. www.copleyinn.com.

Moderate prices and a central location—just behind the Prudential Center—are the strengths of this modest inn. Contained in a four-story brownstone (note that there is no elevator), the rooms are neat, if rather basic (think motel-style Victorian reproductions), but all have kitchenettes. Request one of the large bowfront rooms with a bay window, for a little more space and Old Boston charm.

Staying on Cape Cod, Martha's Vineyard and Nantucket

Properties listed in this section are open year-round, unless otherwise noted.

Luxury

The Wauwinet $$$$$ 32 rooms, 3 cottages

120 Wauwinet Rd., Nantucket. 508-228-0145 or 800-426-8718. www.wauwinet.com. Closed late Oct–early May.

Arguably the finest place to stay on the island, this private, pristine property abuts the Great Point Wildlife Sanctuary, overlooking waves of sea grasses, rolling dunes and the waters of Nantucket Bay. The serene and luxurious resort, nine miles from town, offers a multitude of daily activities, like mountain biking, croquet, tennis, in-room spa treatments, nature hikes, cruises, boating and fishing. It's consistently ranked as one of the top beach hotels in the country, and the resort's **Toppers ($$$$)** restaurant ranks among the island's finest.

White Elephant $$$$$ 66 units

50 Easton St., Nantucket. 800-445-6574. www.whiteelephanthotel.com. Closed mid-Dec–late Apr.

Whitewashed walls and woodwork, crisp linens, wicker furniture, and sweeping harbor views grace this Nantucket landmark. Reeking of casual elegance, the sprawling gray-shingled beach hotel has been a top address for island visitors since the 1920s. Expect attentive service, old-world civilities (the afternoon port and cheese reception) and modern amenities, like high-speed Internet access, in-room spa treatments and a 24-hour concierge.

The Beachside $$$$ 93 rooms

30 North Beach St., Nantucket. 508-228-2241 or 800-322-4433. www.thebeachside.com. Closed mid-Dec–late Apr.

Families love this quiet motel-style property, within walking distance of beaches and historic Main Street. Rooms are clean, bright, and airy and come with a small refrigerator and cable TV. There's an outdoor pool and a free continental breakfast.

Brass Key Guesthouse $$$$ 33 rooms

67 Bradford St., Provincetown, on Cape Cod. 508-487-9005 or 800-842-9858. www.brasskey.com. Closed Jan–Mar.

You'll need to book far in advance for a high-season stay at this guesthouse in bustling Provincetown. The property consists of four 18C and 19C houses and three cottages, clustered around gardens and a pool. Spacious rooms are individually decorated with period décor and antique furnishings; beds sport luxurious linens and goose-down pillows. Some rooms even have fireplaces, whirlpool tubs, heated towel racks and private decks. The compound sits on a quiet side street, within walking minutes to the hub of P-Town activity.

Moderate

Captain's House Inn $$$ 16 rooms

369-377 Old Harbor Rd., Chatham, on Cape Cod. 508-945-0127 or 800-315-0728. www.captainshouseinn.com.

It's hard to imagine a more romantic place to stay on the Cape than this long-time favorite lodging in Chatham. Consisting of an 1839 Greek Revival home, carriage house and renovated stables, the Captain's House features deluxe rooms, most with canopied beds, fireplaces, double whirlpool baths and modern amenities (Internet access, flat-screen TVs, CD players). There are plenty of public spaces, too; cuddle up next to the fireplace in the sitting room, or relax in the vintage library. Rooms are filled with comfy chairs, period antiques and quality reproductions. Like to relax with a massage? There's an on-site day spa, too, offering a host of body treatments.

Hob Knob Inn $$$ 17 rooms

128 Main St., Edgartown, on Martha's Vineyard. 508-627-9510 or 800-696-2723. www.hobknob.com.

Overlooking historic Edgartown, this adults-only inn (no one under 17 years old permitted) is filled with antiques, fresh flowers and a friendly staff. Rooms are drenched in light, with floral fabrics, crisp white linens and comforters, and fluffy down pillows. Nice touches include the full breakfast, on-site exercise and massage rooms, and sauna.

Jared Coffin House $$$ 60 rooms

29 Broad St., Nantucket. 508-228-2400. www.jaredcoffinhouse.com.

You can't miss this three-story 1845 brick mansion in the center of town. If you like staying in impeccably restored and maintained historic hotels, this is the place for you. There's a wide range of room options in five separate houses: the imposing Jared Coffin House, Henry Coffin House, Harrison Gray House, Swain House and Daniel Webster House, all in Nantucket's quaint historic district. All offer colonial charm, some with canopied beds, working fireplaces and Oriental rugs.

Mansion House $$$ 32 rooms

9 Main St., Vineyard Haven, on Martha's Vineyard. 508-693-2200 or 800-332-4112. www.mvmansionhouse.com.

After a day exploring Martha's Vineyard, poking around shops, biking and beaching, the full-service spa at the Mansion House is a welcome site! Relax with a mud body wrap or a massage, join a yoga class, or just relax in the mineral spring pool or sauna. The 5,000-square-foot spa and fitness center is a major draw for this Vineyard Haven property, as are the spacious rooms, award-winning restaurant, **Zephrus ($$$)**, and friendly owners. A $10-million restoration project was completed in 2003, after a fire swept the historic 1794 hotel. Today, it remains a landmark and favorite among island locals and visitors alike.

Inexpensive

Captain Freeman Inn $$ 12 rooms

15 Breakwater St., Brewster, on Cape Cod. Closed Mon–Wed in Jan & Feb. 508-896-7481 or 800-843-4664. www.captainfreemaninn.com.

Loyal guests are hoping this lovely inn on the Outer Cape doesn't change much under the hands of new innkeepers Donna and Peter Amadeo, coming up on their third season at the helm. So far, so good. The immaculately kept inn features a lovely wrap-around porch, and spacious rooms decorated with canopied beds, pretty country lace, and floral fabrics and wallcoverings. Flower and herb gardens surround the outdoor pool area, and it's a short walk to Breakwater Beach on Cape Cod Bay. The six Luxury Rooms come equipped with two-person whirlpool tubs and fireplaces. Children ages 10 and older are welcome.

Dockside Inn $$ 20 rooms, 2 apartments

9 Circuit Ave, Oak Bluffs, on Martha's Vineyard. 508-693-2966 or 800-245-5979. www.vineyardinns.com/dockside.html.

If you like Victorian frilly, you'll appreciate this large inn, reminiscent of a gingerbread cottage, in the Oak Bluffs' harbor district. Rooms are basic and a bit small, filled with floral and pastel fabrics and wall coverings, all with private baths and cable TV. A complimentary continental breakfast is served on the open-air porch or in the greenhouse. The inn is best for couples, as most rooms have queen-size beds and can only accommodate two people; there's an extra fee for kids under age 12. Families are better accommodated in the inn's three larger suites and two apartments.

Orleans Inn $$ 11 rooms

3 Old County Rd., Orleans, on Cape Cod. 508-255-2222 or 800-863-3039. www.orleansinn.com.

This 1875 sea captain's home is arguably the best bargain on the Cape. Its waterfront location, in desirable Orleans, is tough to beat. Added amenities—cable TV, in-room refrigerators, complimentary breakfast—make Orleans Inn a good value. Rooms are cheery and bright with floral prints and country furnishings; some have fireplaces and water views. Guests have access to the inn's kitchenette area and the waterfront deck, a popular place to relax.

Another Way To Look At It: Hotels By Theme

Looking for the best business hotels in Boston? The best hotels to take tea? Want to bring Fido along? In the preceding pages, we've organized the properties by price category, so below we've broken them out by theme to help you plan your trip. Hotels are in Boston, unless otherwise noted.

Closest Hotels to Fenway Park
Eliot Hotel *(p 119)*
Hotel Commonwealth *(p 119)*

Easy on the Budget
Captain Freeman Inn (Cape Cod) *(p 124)*
Chandler Inn Hotel *(p 120)*
Copley Inn *(p 121)*
Dockside Inn (Martha's Vineyard) *(p 124)*
Orleans Inn (Cape Cod) *(p 124)*

For Business Travelers
XV Beacon *(p 115)*
Beacon Hill Hotel and Bistro *(p 118)*
Four Seasons Boston *(p 114)*
Langham Hotel *(p 117)*
Omni Parker House *(p 120)*
Seaport Hotel *(p 118)*
Westin Copley Place *(p 115)*

For Families
The Beachside (Nantucket) *(p 122)*
Boston Marriott Long Wharf *(p 116)*
John Jeffries House *(p 121)*
Wyndham Boston *(p 121)*

Great for Water Views
Boston Harbor Hotel *(p 115)*
Boston Marriott Long Wharf *(p 116)*
Seaport Hotel *(p 118)*
White Elephant (Nantucket) *(p 122)*

Hippest Décor
Clarendon Square Inn *(p 119)*
Encore *(p 120)*
Hotel @ MIT (Cambridge) *(p 119)*
Hotel Marlowe (Cambridge) *(p 116)*
Nine Zero *(p 117)*
Onyx Hotel *(p 118)*

Hotels near Shopping
Brass Key Guesthouse
    (Cape Cod) *(p 122)*
Charles Hotel (Cambridge) *(p 116)*
Copley Inn *(p 121)*
Harborside Inn *(p 121)*
Lenox Hotel *(p 117)*
Newbury Guest House *(p 121)*

Hotels with History
Brass Key Guesthouse
    (Cape Cod) *(p 122)*
A Cambridge House, Bed and
    Breakfast Inn (Cambridge) *(p 118)*
Fairmont Copley Plaza Hotel *(p 116)*
Harborside Inn *(p 121)*
Hob Knob Inn *(p 123)*
Jared Coffin House
    (Nantucket) *(p 123)*
Jurys Boston Hotel *(p 117)*
Lenox Hotel *(p 117)*
Mansion House
    (Martha's Vineyard) *(p 123)*

Posh Places
XV Beacon *(p 115)*
Four Seasons Hotel Boston *(p 114)*
Lenox Hotel *(p 117)*
Ritz-Carlton, Back Bay *(p 114)*
Ritz-Carlton Boston Common *(p 115)*
The Wauwinet (Nantucket) *(p 122)*

Spa Experiences
Captain's House Inn (Cape Cod) *(p 123)*
Mansion House
    (Martha's Vineyard) *(p 123)*
Millennium Bostonian Hotel *(p 120)*
White Elephant (Nantucket) *(p 122)*

Index

Hotels

Index

Photo Credits

KEY: t=top; tl=top left; tm=top middle; tr=top right; m=middle; b=bottom.

A Cambridge House B&B Inn 118b; American Repertory Theatre 70; Aria 78t; Hamersley's Bistro/Avis Studios 103; Bella Santé 80; Boston Beer Works 76t; Boston Center for the Arts 69t; Boston Children's Museum 62t; Boston Harbor Cruises 55; Boston Harbor Fest 57, 67b; Boston Parks & Recreation Dept.: C. Elena Houghton 51, Karen Sparacio 52, Katherine Higgins 67m; Boston Pops/Miro Vintoniv 68; Boston Public Library 40; Boston's Fourth of July 9t, 58; Cape Cod Chamber of Commerce/Sarah Musumeci 89, 90m; Captain Freeman Inn 124t; Centre Street Bistro 111t; Clarendon Square Inn 119t; ©Comstock 108b; Copley Inn 121b; DCR/©Kindra Clineff 56; Dept. of Conservation & Recreation 61; Downtown Crossing Association 31, 74; Encore/Reinhold Mahler 120b; Fairmont Hotels 78b, 114-115, 116m, 125tr; Falmouth Chamber of Commerce 88b; Finale 107m, 113tl; Fog Island Cafe 112t; Four Seasons Hotels 102-103; Freedom Trail Foundation 34, 38, 43t; Gibson House Museum 49

Greater Boston CVB/FAYFOTO, Inc: 4t, 4m, 6m, 6b, 7m, 8t, 8b, 9m, 9b, 18-19, 21, 24b, 26, 29b, 35, 41, 50, 54, 60t, 72, 73, 84, 96.

Photographic Services HUAM ©President and Fellows of Harvard College 85t; Harvest 104b, 113tr; Heritage Museums & Gardens, Sandwich 88t; Historic Urban Plans 20; Hob Knob Inn 123b; Hotel Commonwealth 119b; ©2003ImageDJ Corp. 81; ©Isabella Stewart Gardner Museum, Boston 6t, 44, 45; John F. Kennedy Library Foundation 48; Kimpton Group 116b, 118t, 125tl; Kingfish Hall 105t; Legal Sea Foods 108t; Lenox Hotel 117m; Mamma Maria 105m, 113tm; Martha's Vineyard Chamber of Commerce: Peter Simon 92, Robert Schellhammer 93; Mary Baker Eddy Library 24m; Massachusetts Turnpike Authority 43b.

MICHELIN: ©Brigitta L. House 76b, 109, 110b, 112m; Mills Gallery/Laura Donaldson 69b; MIT Museum 85m; MLB Pressbox 66; ©Museum of Fine Arts, Boston: 46, *The Daughters of Edward Darley Boit*, 1882 by John Singer Sargent 47; Museum of Science 63; Nantucket Island Resorts 5b, 122, 123m, 125tm; ©National Park Service 4b, 8m, 32, 36, 37, 39, 82, 90t, 97, 101m; New England Aquarium/Norman Katz 64; Newbury Guest House 121m; Nine Zero Hotel 117b; Old Sturbridge Village/Thomas Neill 95t; Olives 105b; Orleans Inn 124b; Omni Parker House 120m; Peabody Essex Museum, Salem 7t, 100; ©Peter Vanderwarker 5t, 22, 25, 53; ©PhotoDisc 7b, 95b, 99, 101t, 107b, 112b; Plimoth Plantation 98; Puppet Showplace Theatre 62b; Rails-to-Trails Conservancy 59; Regattabar 79b; Rialto 104t; Roxy 79t; Sfoglia 111m; Sonsie 106t; Starwood Hotels & Resorts 115; The Pearl/Wayne E. Chinnock 110t; The Rack 77; Tremont 647: 106b; Trinity Church 42; USS Constitution Museum 65; Wang Center for the Performing Arts 71; www.aview.com 30; www.NorthEndBoston.com 3, 5m, 28, 29t, 75; www.paddleboston.com 60b.

Cover photos − Front Cover: ©Alan Schein/Corbis. Front small left: Greater Boston CVB/FAYFOTO, Inc. Front small right: Greater Boston CVB/FAYFOTO, Inc. Back Cover: ©Jessica Rinaldi/Reuters/Corbis.